I0407668

Effective Leadership for Supply Chain Management

Dr. Adeel Zeerak

Copyright © 2023 Dr. Adeel Zeerak
All rights reserved

ISBN – 13: 979-8-8572-3161-6

DEDICATION

This book is dedicated to all professionals in the field of supply chain management

ACKNOWLEDGEMENTS

I am thankful to all those who have helped or guided me in any manner in the writing or publishing of this book.

I am also thankful to all my teachers including Mr. Aslam Mustafa who introduced to me the field of supply chain management and motivated me to earn the CSCP and CISCOM certifications.

I am thankful to my father, Abdul Hafeez Qureshi (late), who played a great role in my upbringing and education.

My mother, Raisa Khanam Nighat, whose prayers, guidance, and encouragement have given me the strength to pursue my endeavors.

My other family members including my wife, Dr. Zunairah Rais, and my two wonderful sons, Ahmed Zeerak Qureshi and Muhammad Zeerak Qureshi, who are always a source of inspiration for me.

Dr. Adeel Zeerak

TABLE OF CONTENTS

PREFACE

Organizations throughout the world have recognized the importance of managing their supply chains effectively and efficiently to gain a competitive advantage in the marketplace. A supply chain is a complex phenomenon associated with multiple functions, organizations, and processes to deliver goods and services to customers. Numerous professionals have chosen the field of supply chain management as their professional career. In addition to other relevant skills, effective leadership skills are also very important in the field of supply chain management. This is because supply chain professionals need to deal with numerous individuals inside and outside their organizations to plan, operate, and control their supply chains. This requirement of leadership skills for supply chain professionals becomes even more significant in the case of supply chain professionals working in channel master organizations.

This book explores the importance of leadership in the context of supply chain management. The book is mostly based on the literature review and the research that I conducted during my Ph.D. studies in International Leadership. My research was based on the two streams of knowledge which are supply chain management and leadership. After an initial study of these two key topics, the two streams of knowledge were then merged to have additional valuable insights regarding the significance of effective leadership in managing the supply chains. I researched the desirable traits and behaviors of supply chain managers in manufacturing organizations. My research findings are presented in this book along with other valuable information about leading the supply chains. I believe that the information provided in this book will be helpful to aspiring supply chain professionals, supply chain-related professional bodies, universities offering supply chain courses, and people involved in research related to supply chain management.

Dr. Adeel Zeerak

Chapter 1

ESSENTIALS OF SUPPLY CHAIN MANAGEMENT

I have noticed that the term 'Supply Chain Management' is becoming more and more deeply embedded into the vocabulary of organizational managers; nevertheless, its true concept is not very well understood even by many professionals. Many people confuse the term supply chain management with terms like logistics management, distribution management, transportation management, supply management, and procurement management. All these terms are related to supply chain management but we cannot confine supply chain management to any of these concepts. I know a few organizations that just changed the name of their 'purchasing' department to 'supply chain management' department to give it a newer look without any change in the actual functioning of the department. I have even noticed a few people holding senior management positions in organizations including those in the position of a CEO who are not clear about the term 'supply chain management'.

It is therefore necessary to understand the right concept of a supply chain before proceeding towards the advanced concepts discussed in this book related to leadership or supply chain management. Supply chain management is a very broad concept inclusive of numerous branches of the business including all the aforementioned areas of business activity. In this chapter, I will build the true concept of supply chain management for the reader so that this concept can be later used in subsequent chapters of this book.

WHAT IS A SUPPLY CHAIN

Figure 1 shows the supply chain of a popular household drink that is tea. Consumers buy tea from retail outlets. The retailers get the tea for their shops from the tea wholesalers or distributors. The distributors get the tea from the tea blending and packaging plant. This is the main plant that owns the brand name of a tea. The blending plant buys the tea leaves at tea auctions or from tea brokers. The tea brokers get the tea leaves from the tea plantation sites with adjacent tea leaves processing units. The other major purchase of the tea blending plant is from the producer of packaging material. The packaging material factory buys paper/board from paper and board manufacturers. The packaging material factory also buys chemicals/ink from the chemicals and ink producers. Although the supply chain has a definite end on the consumer (end-user) side the chain will go on the supplier side. For example, even a tea plantation site has its own suppliers like the supplier of fertilizer, etc. However, for illustration and definition purposes, the supply chain of any product is ended at the raw material production stage like in this case, at the stage of tea plantation.

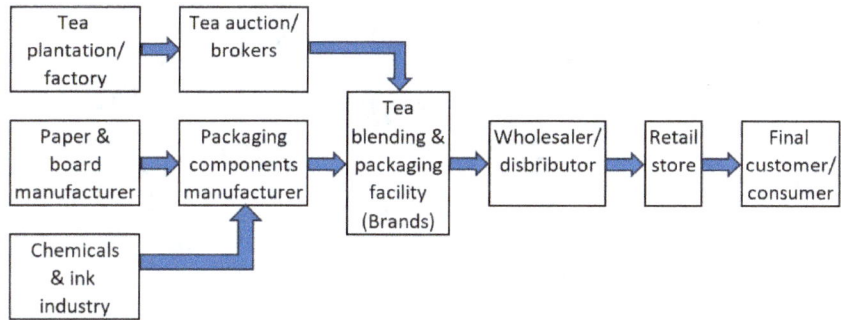

Figure 1: Supply chain of tea

APICS dictionary (2016) defined supply chain as, "The global network used to deliver products and services from raw materials to end customers through an engineered flow of information, physical distribution, and cash" (p. 183). Chopra and Meindl (2013) write, "A supply chain consists of all parties involved, directly or indirectly, in fulfilling a customer request" (p. 19). Thus, a supply chain of a product includes many organizations like manufacturers, suppliers, logistics providers, warehouses, wholesalers, and retailers. Figure 2 shows a schematic diagram for a computer supply chain consisting of various organizations contributing to the production and sale of computers. This supply chain consists of silicon producers, integrated circuits producers, printed circuit board producers, computer assembler, distributors, and the retailer.

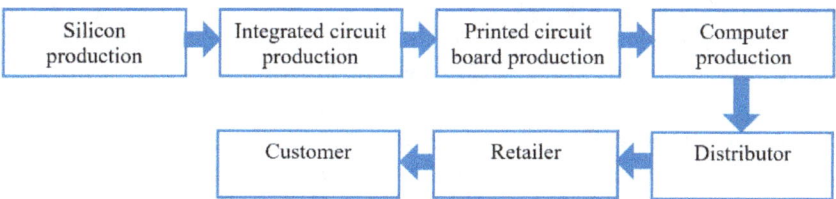

Figure 2: Supply chain of a computer

As depicted in Figure 3, a supply of a product is a complex network that may consist of several suppliers, multiple production facilities, multiple warehouses, and multiple retailers. There can be multiple sales channels for a product including physical shops, company websites, and online marketplaces. These days however online selling is becoming more and more popular in many product categories.

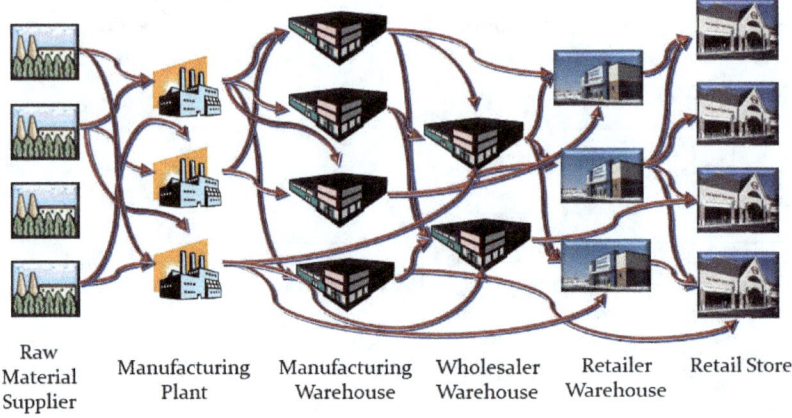

| Raw Material Supplier | Manufacturing Plant | Manufacturing Warehouse | Wholesaler Warehouse | Retailer Warehouse | Retail Store |

Figure 3: Integrated supply chain network

Supply chains exist for both manufacturing and service organizations. Within each organization, a supply chain includes all functional areas involved in receiving and filling the customer order, including sales and, marketing, operations, distribution, finance, and customer service. Thus, the concept of supply chain is very broad and it involves various functional areas within an organization and various organizations contributing to the supply of a product or service in the market.

FOUR FLOWS IN SUPPLY CHAINS

As an analogy, if we consider a supply chain as a pipeline consisting of various organizations in a supply chain then four things are flowing through that pipe. The first flow is information flowing among supply chain partner organizations. The direction of information flow is both upstream to downstream and from downstream to upstream, that is, the flow in both directions. The primary cash or funds flow is from downstream to upstream in the form of payments for products and services bought from the suppliers of each organization. The primary product flow is from upstream to downstream. The reverse product flow is from downstream to upstream which may be due to many reasons like product returns, recycling, refilling, refurbishment, repairs, etc. Figure 4 depicts these four flows in a supply chain with examples of each flow. One major objective of supply chain management is to effectively and efficiently manage these four types of flows in a supply chain.

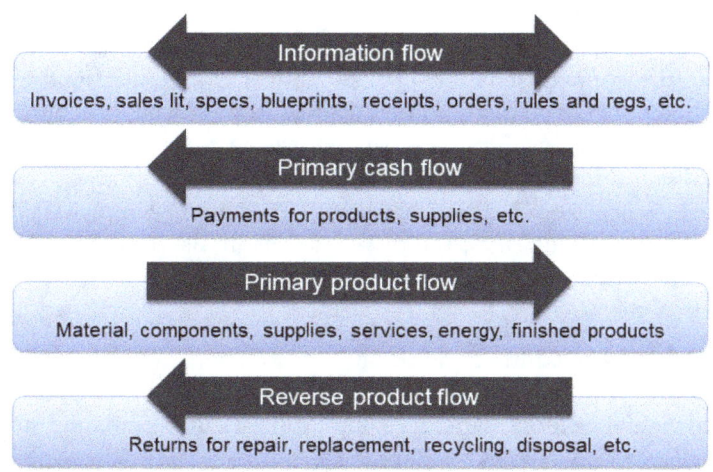

Figure 4: Four flows in a supply chain

MANAGING SUPPLY CHAINS

Historically, managerial attention was devoted to issues that were internal to companies, and specialists in procurements, sales, and logistics were assigned to 'deal' with all external entities like suppliers and customers. The first major change in this perspective can be traced back to the explosive growth of Just-in-Time concepts in the 1970s. With this shift, suppliers and customers began to be viewed as partners who shared mutually linked destinies. Great emphasis was then placed on the trust between partners and many formal boundary mechanisms, such as the receiving/inspection activity of incoming parts, were either changed or eliminated. As the partnership concept among the organizations grew, many other changes in the relationship were experienced including mutual analysis of cost reduction, mutual product design, and enhanced information flows. The term supply chain management eventually evolved. In the 1990s the term supply chain became part of the vocabulary of some organizational CEOs, COOs, CFOs, and CIOs (Coyle, Langley, Gibson & Novack, 2017). Ultimately, organizations in the supply chain started to be considered as extended enterprise with joint destinies.

The concept of supply chain management further expanded with the accelerated advancement in computer capability and associated software applications as well as the rise in global competition. Shorter product life cycles in many industries forced companies to not only become more agile and flexible but also to enhance the communication of changes and needs to suppliers and distributors. It is said that a chain is as strong as its weakest link. This also holds in the context of supply chains. Almost all organizations rely heavily upon their suppliers and distribution partners to produce and sell their products effectively and efficiently. This is because any disturbance in its supply-side or distribution side can severely hamper the ability of an organization to produce and sell its products. Therefore, Supply Chain professionals view the working of all the organizations in a supply chain as a single extended enterprise with linked goals.

APICS dictionary (2016) defines supply chain management as, "the design, planning, execution, control, and monitoring of supply chain activities with the objective of creating net value, building a competitive infrastructure, leveraging worldwide logistics, synchronizing supply and demand, and measuring performance globally." This definition elaborates on many aspects that are important for managing supply chains. Firstly, the definition talks about the various management tasks including planning, executing, monitoring, and controlling various activities related to supply chain management. The definition starts with the designing of the supply chain network and ends with the monitoring and controlling of the supply chain activities during routine operations. Designing supply chains involves activities like deciding upon the location of the various facilities like manufacturing plants and warehouses; designing an effective transportation network; selecting suppliers and other supply chain partner organizations, etc.

The definition also talks about other important aspects of supply chain management like creating value through supply chains for the customer, building a competitive infrastructure, making use of available worldwide logistics, and performance management using supply chain-related metrics. The definition also talks about a very important aspect of managing the supply chains which is synchronizing the supply and demand of the product to avoid sales loss or oversupply of a product. Organizations that adopt the concept of supply chain management view the entire set of supply chain activities from the initial phase of raw material production to the final stage of purchase by the consumer as a linked chain of activities.

When faced with supply chain disruptions, proactive and reactive supply chain risk management can in fact make or break a company. A classic example often quoted of supply chain disruption is that of Ericsson and Nokia. A fire erupted at the Philips microchip plant in Albuquerque, New Mexico, in 2000, which simultaneously affected both Nokia and Ericsson. The companies took very different approaches towards the incident, and in hindsight, clearly displayed both how to and how not to handle supply chain disruptions. The plant supplied chips to both Ericsson and Nokia and the smoke and water damage from the small and easily contained fire contaminated millions of chips — almost the plant's entire stock. Nokia acted swiftly and moved to tie up spare capacity at other Philips plants and every other supplier they could find. They even re-engineered some of their phones so they could secure chips from other Japanese and American suppliers. Ericsson, meanwhile, accepted early assurances that the fire was unlikely to cause a big problem and settled down complacently to wait it out. By the time they realized their mistake it was too late. Ericsson, just a few years earlier, had decided to buy key components from a single source to simplify its supply chain, and it now had to face the bitter realization that it had no other source of supply. Nokia had obtained them all by now. Ericsson lost many months of production, and hence many sales in a booming market that would now be dominated by Nokia. Eventually, Ericsson had to merge with Sony in order to survive.

Over the last few years, a body of knowledge has evolved to train professionals in the field of Supply Chain Management. Typical topics discussed in Supply Chain Management include Management of Business Logistics; Customer and Supplier relationship management; production planning; materials requirement planning (MRP); forecasting; distribution management; warehousing and inventory management; Enterprise Resource Planning (ERP) and other information technology tools. Supply Chain Council (an independent not-for-profit global organization) has developed a Supply Chain Operations Reference (SCOR) model to guide organizations in their supply chain efforts.

CREATING VALUE THROUGH A SUPPLY CHAIN

The supply chain management approach provided organizations an opportunity to reduce costs and enhance revenues through improved execution of processes and by providing superior customer service. There is a purpose behind every well-planned activity. So, what is the purpose of supply chain management? Initially, cost reduction was stated to be the objective of supply chain management. Supply chain professionals, however, felt that this stated objective of cost reduction is a very narrow scope for the discipline of supply chain management. Therefore, it is now asserted that the objective of supply chain management is to create value. This created value is further classified into customer value for the customers, the financial value for the supply chain partner organizations, and the social value for society.

Customer value takes the form of superior goods and services that are valued by the customer. If a customer finds a good or service valuable then he will buy it thus creating financial value in terms of enhanced revenue and profit for all the organizations in a supply chain. And if the supply chain is for a good product (and not for a harmful product like heroin, etc.), then it will benefit the whole society in terms of the availability of goods and services, employment generation, tax generation, import substitution, etc. Thus, organizations in a supply chain must strive to create enhanced customer value, financial value, and social value through their supply chains.

EVOLUTION OF SUPPLY CHAIN MANAGEMENT

Figure 5 shows a typical organogram for an organization in which various departments exist to perform certain functions in an organization. Departments are created to perform certain organizational functions. Typical departments in an organization are production, sales/marketing, finance, maintenance, human resources, administration, and information technology. The CEO is at the top of all the functions overseeing and managing the whole organization. The various functional departments are vertically organized with many levels of executives like general managers, managers, deputy managers, etc. The functions shown in Figure 5 resemble the silos that are used for the storage of materials. In management, these departments are also sometimes referred to as silos especially if there is a lack of coordination and teamwork between the various departments of an organization.

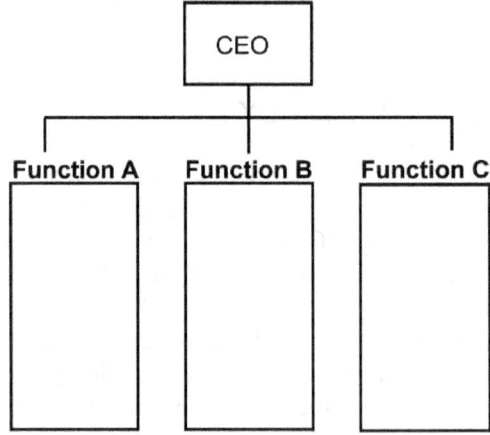

Figure 5: Functional arrangement in a typical organization

Various processes are executed in an organization. Some examples of organizational processes are the customer order fulfillment process, production process, and purchasing process. All these processes involve multiple departments for successful completion. Take the example of the order fulfillment process which starts with the customer placing an order and ends with the receiving of the ordered product by the customer. In this process, multiple departments of an organization will be involved including sales, production planning & control, production, procurement, quality assurance, finance, and logistics. In the same way, every process in an organization is completed only after the involvement of various departments of the organization. In this way, we can say that the functions (departments) of an organization are vertically organized as discussed before whereas organizational processes are conducted horizontally cutting across various departments as shown in Figure 6.

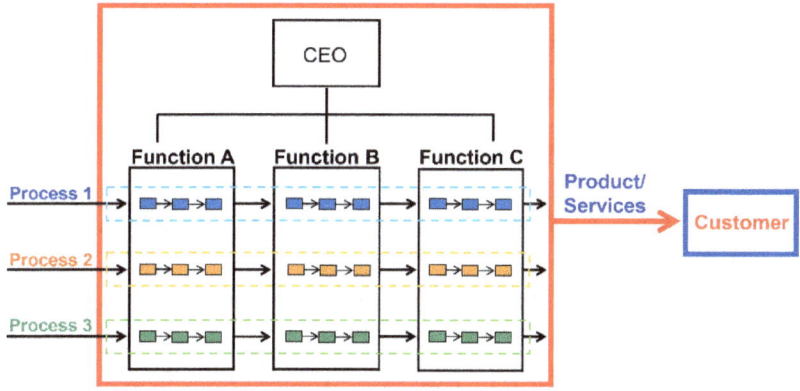

Figure 6: Functions and processes in an organization

Figure 6 shows the importance of teamwork and coordination among various functions of an organization. Thus, the execution quality of any organizational process will enhance only if there is better coordination and teamwork among various departments in an organization involved in a process. By extending the same logic, we can say that the whole supply chain will perform very well if there is coordination and teamwork between the various organizations within a supply chain. These organizations include suppliers, manufacturers, distributors, retailers, etc. This is why a supply chain is considered an extended enterprise that crosses the boundaries of individual firms to span the related activities of all the companies involved in the total supply chain.

Thus, effective supply chain management requires enhanced teamwork not only among the various departments inside the organization but also good teamwork outside the organization among supply chain partner organizations. This enhanced teamwork in a supply chain may however take a few steps starting from improvement within the departmental walls towards a well-coordinated extended enterprise. This evolution towards effective supply chain management may take the following five stages.

STAGE 1: Multiple dysfunction organization

This is the least desirable state of any functioning organization. At this stage, the organization lacks clear internal definitions and goals and has no external links with supply chain partner organizations other than transactional linkages. At this stage, the organization is not being run professionally and proactively even within the departmental walls. That is, there is not even effectiveness and efficiency within the departments. Even individual departments are not functioning professionally in an organization. There is no teamwork and coordination between various departments. The supply chain at this stage is a reactive supply chain instead of being proactive.

STAGE 2: Semi-functional enterprise

This is a level higher than the multiple dysfunction level. At this stage, the organization undertakes initiatives to improve effectiveness, efficiency, and quality within functional areas. The various organizational departments have started to work professionally. For example, the production department is working effectively to produce organizational goods and the marketing department now knows how to promote and sell products effectively. At this stage, while some or all functions engage in initiatives designed to increase efficiency within their departmental walls, there is little or no overlap in decision-making from one department to another. Thus, the teamwork and coordination between various departments in the organization is still not so good. At this stage, the supply chain is called the reactive-efficient supply chain.

STAGE 3: Integrated enterprise

Coordination and teamwork among various departments in an organization improve at this stage of supply chain evolution. The organization breaks down silo walls and brings functional areas together in processes such as sales and operations planning (S&OP) with a focus on companywide processes rather than individual functions. The organization is typically linked together with a single database and a single ERP software. Cross-functional teams like cross-functional design teams are formed for various tasks. Thus, at this stage, there is greater coordination and teamwork among various departments. Organizational internal integration is achieved at this stage and thus it has become now proactive. At this stage, the supply chain is called the proactive-efficient supply chain.

STAGE 4: Extended enterprise

External integration of an organization happens at this stage. The organization links its internal network with the internal networks of selected supply chain partners to improve efficiency, product/service quality, or both. The starting point of this stage is usually one inside/outside partnership that points the way toward the completely networked enterprise. This is the stage at which the supply chain of a product is truly working as an extended enterprise. In fact, according to one definition a supply chain is "an extended enterprise that crosses the boundaries of individual firms to span the related activities of all the companies involved in the total supply chain." (Coyle & Langley, 9e) At this stage, the supply chain is called the strategic driver supply chain.

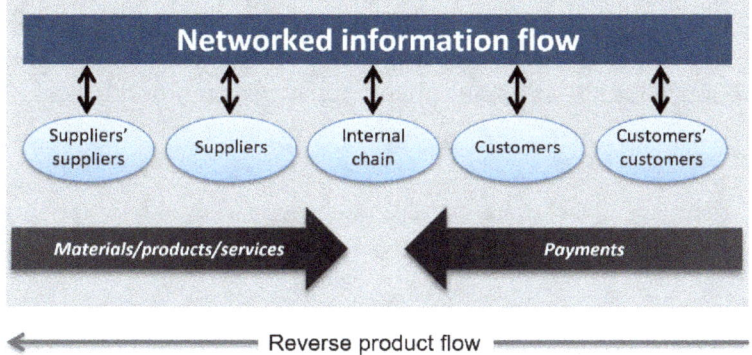

Figure 7: Supply chain as an extended enterprise

STAGE 5: Orchestrated supply chain

This stage of a supply chain is often expressed as a supply chain digital transformation. At this stage, the supply chain involves seamless technology integration, skilled human resources, and teams to leverage technology investments. A supply chain in this stage realizes an actual competitive advantage from becoming better orchestrated than its competitors. It requires more than just seamless technology; it requires skilled leaders and teams who can leverage technologies and adapt quickly to changes. At this stage, the supply chain is called the consistent and systematic supply chain.

CHANNEL MASTER

Better coordination and teamwork amongst firms enable organizations in the supply chain to create better financial value, benefiting each one of them. These firms in a supply chain do not have unified ownership. For example, the suppliers have different ownerships and the manufacturer belongs to a different owner. In the same way, wholesalers and retailers may have different ownership. The question now arises that how can a supply chain be managed effectively in the absence of a single ownership for the whole chain? The answer is that in practice, typically there is a single more professional organization in the supply chain that is called the nucleus firm or the channel master. This organization takes the supply chain management initiative within the supply chain. This channel master or nucleus firm traditionally consisted of large manufacturers that influenced their suppliers and distributors into collaboration for mutual benefit. Examples of a manufacturer as channel master are of Apple Inc. and Toyota Motor Corporation. Nowadays in many industries, the power of the channel master has now shifted towards giant retailers like Walmart. The leadership role of channel master organizations is discussed in detail in chapter 4 of this book.

Chapter 2

ESSENTIALS OF LEADERSHIP

Leadership is mostly viewed as an influencing process for the achievement of certain goals. For example, according to one definition, leadership is, "a process of influencing a group to achieve goals" (Robbins & Mary, 2016, p. 523). Weirich, Cannice and Koontz (2008) defined leadership as "the art or process of influencing people so that they will strive willingly and enthusiastically toward the achievement of group goals" (p. 347). The process of influencing is generally common among the various definitions of leadership. The second common element in the definitions is the achievement of goals. We can therefore conclude leaders are people who achieve certain desired goals using their influencing power as a leader.

MANAGER VERSUS LEADER

Like in my case, you must have also seen numerous fancy one-pagers showing the difference between a manager and a leader or a boss and a leader. If not, you can google some among a wide collection of such documents on the internet. All such documents imply that a leader is somewhat of a superior being as compared to a manager and tries to explain the differences between the two with the help of concepts like vision, change, risks, motivation, relationships, coaching, short and long-term orientation, etc. Although I do not fully agree with many of such comparisons, these comparisons may be a good tool to inspire a manager to become a good leader or some sort of superior manager.

If we look into what leadership scholars have to say about it, then we see two distinct opinions regarding this issue. Some leadership scholars have differentiated leaders from managers concerning the change they bring about. According to them, leaders bring about some positive change whereas managers maintain the status quo and only motivate people to work effectively. This implies that if a person is a good manager then he or she is not a leader unless he or she brings about some positive change. Leadership scholars like Zalennik, Kotter, and Nohria belong to such a group of scholars who link leadership with change. Others disagree with this dichotomy and assert that good managers are also leaders if they are influencing others to follow them. This implies that good managers may also be good leaders and leadership may or may not necessarily involve some change. An example of such a scholar is Lorsch who explains, "… an individual is a leader whether she is a senior executive leading an effort to change the strategic direction of her company or is a supervisor leading a group of workers on an assembly line. … True, she faces different task, organizational, and relationship issues, but the goal is the same – influencing others to follow her."

It is also witnessed in the real business world that mostly the term manager like deputy manager, manager, or general manager as formal designations are used for professionals at various organizational levels. As a formal designation, the term leader is very rarely used. And the organizations expect these managers to display good leadership qualities. For this purpose, a lot of training budget is consumed by organizations on leadership trainings of their managers. So, what do we conclude? We conclude that there is a difference of opinion among scholars over this matter. As managers, we should try to become good leaders as well and must try to get the best from the leadership development efforts employed on us by our organizations. We should strive to simultaneously become good managers as well as effective leaders. Most of us are already in managerial positions, therefore we must make a conscious effort to become effective leaders. In the same way, supply chain managers should also strive to become good leaders as they may have to influence the whole supply chain to achieve the supply chain goals of their organizations.

SCHOLARLY EFFORTS TO UNDERSTAND LEADERSHIP

The topic of leadership is studied by scholars from various disciplines including organizational behavior, psychology, clinical science, economics, sociology, history, and political science. Each discipline used its peculiar approach to study the leadership phenomenon (Nohria & Khurana, 2010). This book, however, has utilized the organizational behavior approach to study the effective leadership qualities of supply chain managers. The reason is that; it is the organizational behavior approach that is mostly used by the authors of books on management that are recommended at business schools. Therefore, the organizational behavior approach to understand the leadership phenomenon is known by most of the university graduates who are later employed in the business world in leadership positions including in the field of supply chain management.

Glynn and DeJordy (2010) researched the organizational behavior approach to leadership study. They based their research on leadership articles published in three renowned journals of organizational behavior during the 50 years. The time period of the studied publications was from 1957 to 2007. They found that there were three main approaches in organizational behavior literature to study leadership. These approaches were trait approach, behavior approach, and contingency approach. According to their research, some leadership papers were also published in organizational behavior journals based on the theories of change, influence, and charisma. A brief description of the three major approaches to study leadership is mentioned in the following text.

TRAIT APPROACH TO LEADERSHIP STUDY

The trait approach to leadership study was the earliest approach to understanding the leadership phenomenon in the organizational behavior approach (Glynn & DeJordy, 2010). Zaccaro (2007) defined leaders' traits as "relatively coherent and integrated patterns of personal characteristics, reflecting a range of individual differences, that foster consistent leadership effectiveness across a variety of group and organizational situations" (p. 7). The trait approach assumed that there are some common inherent qualities in leaders that distinguish them from the non-leaders. As a result, many trait theories of leadership appeared that were earlier referred to as the Great Man theories of leadership. The leaders' inherent qualities that were studied in the trait approach were extraordinary personality attributes, abilities, skills, or physical characteristics (Glynn & DeJordy, 2010).

The earliest trait theories that focused on the leader as a person were not so successful. Leaders' traits explored in the earlier studies in the 1920s and 1930s were physical stature, appearance, social class, emotional stability, speech fluency, and social ability. However, later trait theories that focused on the leadership process rather than the person were more successful (Robbins & Mary, 2016). The trait approach to leadership is still applicable. However, it is asserted that having some desirable traits alone is not enough for effective leadership. Traits can be considered as only a precondition for effective leadership. Other than traits, leaders need to apply appropriate behavior for their leadership success (Kirkpatrick & Locke, 1991). Kirkpatrick and Locke

(1991) in their study identified the six major traits in a leader that made them different from the non-leaders. These six major traits of a leader are mentioned in Table 1 with a brief explanation of each trait.

DRIVE	LEADERSHIP MOTIVATION
• Exhibit a high level of effort. • Have a high desire for achievement. • Energetic. • Show initiative. • Persistent in activities.	• Desire to lead. • Willingness to take responsibility.
HONESTY & INTEGRITY	SELF-CONFIDENCE
• Built a trusting relationship with followers. • Truthful. • High consistency between words & deeds.	• Absence of self-doubt. • Convinced at the rightness of their goals & decisions. • Emotional stability.
COGNITIVE ABILITY	KNOWLEDGE OF THE BUSINESS
• Intelligence. • Gather, synthesize & interprets information. • Good in problem-solving & decision making.	• In-depth knowledge about organization & industry. • Knowledge about technical matters.

Table 1: Six major traits of a leader

Kirkpatrick & Locke also mentioned the additional traits of charisma, creativity/originality, and flexibility for leadership effectiveness. However, according to them, these later three traits were comparatively less significant for the leaders as compared to the six identified major traits. According to another study, the trait is leadership charisma is more important for political leaders as compared with organizational leaders.

A related change in the trait approach resulted in a skills and competencies approach to leadership study that still focused on leaders' qualities (Luthans, 2008). Germain (2012) explored the relationship between leadership traits and expert traits. For the research, Germain consulted the expertise literature and leadership theories present in the literature. He found many areas of commonality between leadership traits and expert skills. He found overlapping in the areas like ambition, judgment, outgoing nature, self-confidence, knowledge, problem-solving skills, intuition, ability to deduce, ability to improve, charisma, and drive.

Tubbs and Schulz (2006) developed a taxonomy of the global leadership competencies and meta-competencies. They mentioned seven meta-competencies and fifty competencies in their taxonomy of leadership competencies. The meta-competencies identified were: Understanding the big picture, attitudes are everything, leadership the driving force, communication the leader's voice, innovation, and creativity, leading change, and teamwork and followership. Tubbs and Schulz grouped various competencies under the umbrella of these seven identified meta-competencies. The paper suggested that some aspects of leadership are fixed from a young age, whereas other competencies can be developed in leaders at the later stages of their life.

Serial Number	Metacompetency
I	Understanding the big picture
II	Attitudes are everything
III	Leadership - the driving force
IV	Communications - the leader's voice
V	Innovation & creativity
VI	Leading change
VII	Teamwork & followership

Table 2: Leadership meta-competencies by Tubbs & Schulz

Zaccaro (2007) proposed a model for leader attributes and leader performance. The model classified the leadership traits into two groups, that are distal attributes and proximal attributes. Figure 8 shows the model presented by Zaccaro (2007) for leader attributes and leader performance. According to the model, proximal attributes are more related to the leaders' operating environment as compared to the distal attributes. The model included cognitive abilities, personality, motives, and values in the distal attributes list, whereas social appraisal skills, problem-solving skills, and expertise/tacit knowledge were in the proximal attributes list. According to the model, these leadership attributes result in a leader process that in turn results in leader emergence, leader effectiveness, and leader advancement and promotion.

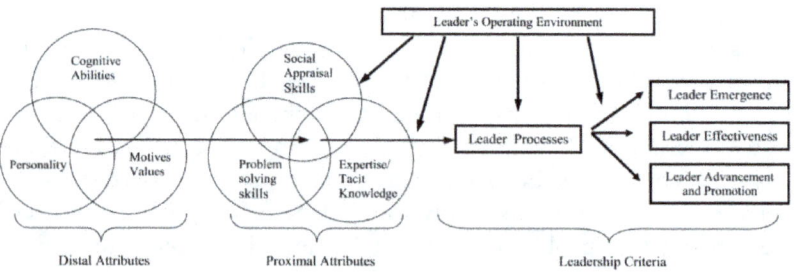

Figure 8: Model of leader attributes and leader performance by Zaccaro

The trait approach to leadership study was dominant in the early periods of leadership research. However, later the trait approach was disdained due to its inability to find common leadership traits and its inability to account for situational factors for leaders. Recently there is a re-emergence of the trait approach to leadership study driven by conceptual, methodological, and statistical sophistication in the field of research (Zaccaro, 2007).

BEHAVIOR APPROACH TO LEADERSHIP STUDY

The behavior approach to leadership study asserted that leadership effectiveness depends upon how a leader behaves. This approach identified various leadership behaviors in an attempt to find out the best behavior for a leader for leadership effectiveness. Lewin, Lippitt, and White (1939) were the pioneers of the behavior approach to leadership study (Glynn & DeJordy, 2010). They identified three leadership styles, that are autocratic style, democratic style, and laissez-faire style. In the autocratic style of leadership, a leader tends to dictate work methods, make unilateral decisions, and limit employee participation. In the democratic style of leadership, a leader tends to involve employees in decision-making, delegates authority and uses feedback as an opportunity for coaching employees. In the laissez-faire style, a leader generally lets the group make decisions and complete the work in whatever way it sees fit (Robbins & Mary, 2016).

Yukl, Gordon, and Taber (2002) asserted that early research on behavioral theories of leadership was mostly based on a two-factor model. These studies included Ohio State studies and the University of Michigan studies on leadership behavior. Ohio State research identified two basic styles of leadership that are, initiating structure and consideration. In the initiating structure style, a leader defines and structures his or her role and the role of group members in search of goal attainment. In the consideration leadership style, a leader had job relationships characterized by mutual trust and respect for group members' ideas and feelings (Robbins & Mary, 2016). University of Michigan research identified two leadership styles that are production-oriented and employee-oriented. In the production-oriented style of leadership, a leader tends to emphasize the technical and task aspects of the job, is concerned mainly with groups' tasks, and regards group members as the means to achieve goals. In the employee-oriented leadership style, a leader emphasizes interpersonal relationships and takes a personal interest in the needs of the followers (Robbins & Mary, 2016).

With time leadership, scholars became more interested in the way leaders initiate and implement change in organizations. The recent theories of transformational and charismatic leadership included change-oriented behaviors that are relevant to leadership effectiveness (Barrasa, 2003). Thus, Yukl, Gordon and Taber (2002) developed a three-dimensional taxonomy of leadership behaviors that included change behavior. They developed a taxonomy of three meta-categories of leaders' behavior that are task behavior, relations behavior, and change behavior. The meta-categories developed by Yukl, Gordon and Taber seemed to be more comprehensive than the University of Michigan or Ohio State studies as they included an important dimension of change, which is very relevant to the study leadership. Table 3 shows the hierarchical taxonomy of leader behavior as developed by Yukl, Gordon and Taber.

TASK BEHAVIOR
   Plan short term activities
   Clarify task objectives & role expectations
   Monitor operations & performance

RELATIONS BEHAVIOR
   Provide support & encouragement
   Provide recognition for achievements & contributions
   Develop member skills & confidence
   Consult with members when making decisions
   Empower members to take initiative in problem solving

CHANGE BEHAVIOR
   Monitor the external environment
   Propose an innovative strategy or new vision
   Encourage innovative thinking
   Take risks to promote necessary changes

Table 3: Hierarchical taxonomy of leadership behaviors

CONTINGENCY APPROACH TO LEADERSHIP STUDY

Contingency leadership theories asserted that the effective leadership style or behavior should vary according to the situation or the context in which a leader is operating. According to the contingency approach, there is no single leadership style that is effective in all situations. Therefore, a leader must apply suitable behavior that matches the situation at hand. Various contingency theories have emerged with time that had defined various leadership situations and recommended a particular leadership behavior for each situation. One of the most quoted contingency theories of leadership in management training programs is Hersey and Blanchard's situational leadership theory. According to this theory, the best leadership style depends upon the readiness of the followers being led.

OTHER APPROACHES

There evolved some other approaches to leadership study in the organizational behavior literature. These theories are related to change, influence, and charisma. These theories are mostly built on and are the extension of the previous works related to trait, behavior, and contingency approaches of leadership study (Glynn & DeJordy, 2010). Some newer theories of leadership have closely related leadership to the change process. They considered a leader as a catalyst of change. The process of change by leadership is of two kinds that are transactional or transformational (Glynn & DeJordy, 2010). Robbins and Mary (2016) defined transactional leaders as "leaders who lead primarily by using social exchanges (or transactions)" (p. 532). Whereas, they defined transformational leaders as "leaders who stimulate and inspire (transform) followers to achieve extraordinary outcomes" (p. 532). Transformational leaders inspire their followers to develop self-interest for the well-being of the organization. The research evidence demonstrated the superiority of transformational leadership over transactional leadership. However, the two styles of leadership should not be considered mutually exclusive and opposite of each other. Leaders build transformational leadership on top of their transactional leadership (Robbins & Mary, 2016).

A leader's power is a means of influencing others. Authority is the right to influence others by virtue of one's position (Business Edge, n.d). The five sources of a leader's power are legitimate power, coercive power, reward power, expert power, and referent power. Legitimate power in a leader comes from his or her formal position in the organizational hierarchy. The coercive power of a leader is his or her ability to punish or control his or her followers. The reward power of a leader comes from his or her ability to provide rewards to the followers. Expert power in a leader comes by virtue of his or her expertise, skills, and knowledge. Referent power arises because of a leader's desirable resources or personal traits. Leaders use a combination of available sources of power available to them to influence others (Robbins & Mary, 2016).

Here in this chapter, I have very briefly discussed the topic of leadership. In case you are interested to know more about leadership then you can consult my book "Become An Effective Corporate Leader". This book is available at www.amazon.com.

Chapter 3

ROLE OF LEADERSHIP IN SUPPLY CHAIN MANAGEMENT

In the previous two chapters, we have learned the essential concepts of supply chain management and leadership. In this chapter, I will combine these two concepts that is I will discuss leadership in the context of supply chain management. Context is important for leadership study as a leadership style may vary significantly depending on the context in which the leader is operating. The contingency theories of leadership have tried to recommend various leadership styles for various situations and contexts. However, there is still a need to study leadership qualities for various specific contexts as asserted by Hackman (2010) during his closing speech following two days of discussions on leadership at the Harvard Business School centennial colloquium on advancing leadership. Hackman asserted: "Context is indeed a challenge: What are we to do about the radical differences in the context of leadership for, say, a Boy Scout troop, a senior leadership team, a professional string quartet, and a product development team in an industrial firm? Could it be true that leadership operates the same way in these radically different contexts? Indeed, does leadership even mean the same thing across contexts? The two most common suggestions for dealing with contextual differences are to develop contingency theories that take account of context and to develop mid-range theories that are tailored for certain contexts but that are not presumed or expected to apply to others." (as cited in Nohria & Khurana, 2010, p. 111).

In line with Hackman's (2010) advice, I will discuss in detail leadership in the context of supply chain management where a supply chain manager is working for managing the supply chain in a manufacturing organization. His or her situation or context is very different from other contexts like a manager working in a hospital environment or a manager working on a project in a construction environment. Each context demands a varying emphasis on various leadership traits and behaviors for leadership effectiveness. Therefore, it is necessary to study leadership in the context of supply chain management.

LEADERSHIP IN SUPPLY CHAIN MANAGEMENT

Effective supply chain management requires utilization and cooperation of resources among the various organizations in a supply chain and it requires organizations to participate in cooperative activities to reach a win-win situation for all. A supply chain does not have single ownership of the whole chain as it consists of many organizations working together to produce and deliver goods and services. All the firms in a supply chain do not possess equal power to influence the various supply chain processes. Usually, there exists a single dominant firm in the supply chain, called a nucleus organization or a channel master that aligns supply chain best practices throughout the chain. Such a nucleus firm or channel master therefore mostly takes the leadership role within a supply chain to influence other organizations in applying supply chain management best practices for the benefit of the whole chain (APICS, 2019).

Many organizations have developed supply chain teams on a full-time or part-time basis for effective and efficient management of their supply chain activities. Some organizations have created dedicated supply chain departments for this purpose. Whether working on a full-time or part-time basis, supply chain managers need to design, coordinate and align various supply chain-related activities not only within their organizations but also among other partner organizations in their supply chains (APICS, 2011). Supply chain managers, therefore, need to display excellent leadership skills to influence other entities and professionals to align and coordinate supply chain activities throughout the chain. This is especially true for supply chain managers working in channel master organizations.

Supply chain managers need to influence professionals working in various departments in their organizations like operations, warehousing, procurement, and information technology and they also need to influence outside entities like transporters, suppliers, and distributors. Therefore, various scholars and bodies of knowledge on supply chain management have emphasized the leadership qualities of people involved in supply chain management. Two examples are the APICS (2011) body of knowledge developed for the Certified Supply Chain Professional (CSCP) certification and the book on supply chain management by Coyle, Langley, Gibson and Novack (2017).

Managing supply chains required skillful management and strong leadership skills (APICS, 2011). In their research, Crook, Giunipero, Reus,

Handfield and Williams (2008) explored the antecedents and outcomes of effective supply chains. Among other antecedents, their paper also identified leadership skills in the category of broad skills and knowledge as one of the antecedents of supply chain effectiveness. The Supply chain manager competency model developed by APICS (2014) also identified certain managerial and leadership competencies for supply chain managers. Thus, effective leadership is one important factor in supply chain management for effective supply chain outcomes. Supply chain executives are now being elevated to strategic roles in many organizations. Managing supply chains require people with the right skills in leadership roles. Supply chain leaders need to be critical thinkers and problem solvers. They must be able to see the big picture, develop integrated solutions, establish contingency plans, and communicate the vision (Coyle, Langley, Gibson & Novack, 2017). After looking at the importance of supply chain management, some experts have even predicted that future CEOs will come from the area of supply chain management (Mikhail, 2018).

Although the body of knowledge developed for supply chain management stressed the importance of leadership skills in managing supply chains, there is a lack of knowledge regarding the specific leadership qualities required in the context of supply chain management. Most of the supply chain literature has discussed the technical aspects of running the supply chains, but surprisingly there is very little knowledge about the managerial and leadership aspects of running supply chains. This book is mostly based on my research during my Ph.D. studies to identify the effective leadership qualities of supply chain managers in terms of required leadership traits and behaviors in manufacturing organizations for effective supply chain outcomes.

IMPORTANCE OF LEADERSHIP FOR SUPPLY CHAIN MANAGERS

The first research question for my research was developed to access the importance of leadership qualities for supply chain managers working in manufacturing sector organizations for effective supply chain outcomes. My study confirmed that it is very important for supply chain managers in manufacturing organizations to have good leadership qualities for effective supply chain outcomes. The study revealed the following two reasons for the importance of leadership qualities for supply chain managers working in manufacturing organizations for effective supply chain outcomes:

1. Supply chain management involves internal and external integration in organizations. Internal integration is between various functions of an organization, whereas, external integration involves outside entities like suppliers, logistics providers, and customers. Such internal and external integration efforts require good leadership qualities of supply chain managers. This is because a person with good leadership skills can influence others to seek cooperation to form linkages with inside and outside entities in supply chains.

2. Leadership qualities are required to understand and lead the team involved in managing the supply chains. Professionals from various functional areas within an organization including procurement, production, warehousing, logistics, and sales, are involved in managing supply chain processes for an organization. Therefore, managing or influencing professionals from these functional areas to run the supply chain effectively requires good leadership skills on the part of supply chain managers.

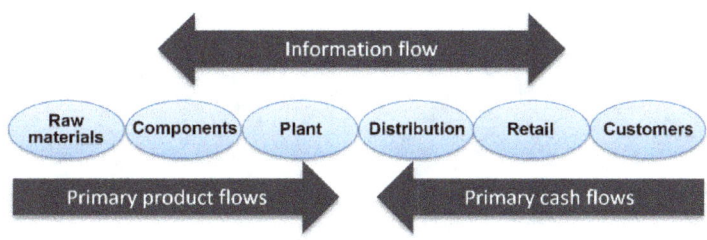

Figure 9: Lateral integration in supply chains

Thus, my research further confirmed the literature review findings, and thus it was concluded that leadership qualities are very important for supply chain managers working in manufacturing organizations for effective supply chain outcomes. Therefore, supply chain managers must strive to improve their leadership skills to enhance their performance as supply chain managers. They need to improve their leadership skills for effective supply chain outcomes. The specific requirements for the leadership skills from them in terms of leadership traits and behaviors are discussed later in chapter 5 of this book. But before discussing those specific leadership skills, I will discuss further the leadership role of channel master organization in managing the supply chains in the next chapter.

Chapter 4

LEADERSHIP ROLE OF CHANNEL MASTERS

Ayers & Odegaard (2008) has defined and elaborated a channel master as, "The single, most powerful company in a supply chain. The channel master dictates the terms of trade for the channel. The presence of a master depends on the nature of the industry and competition. Channel mastery is often the goal of supply chain management programs." (p. 362). A channel master in a supply chain exercises influence over other organizations in the network, often directing activities, technology, and behavior in the supply chain. For example, Walmart as a channel master made it mandatory for all participating suppliers to embrace RFID technology for inventory management (BRASI, 2018). Influence is a characteristic of leadership as leadership is all about influencing others to act in a certain way to achieve certain goals (Yukl, 1989). Therefore, it can be said that a channel master, as an organization, plays the role of a leader for a supply chain network as it influences other organizations to achieve supply chain goals. The leadership role of a channel master becomes even more important and challenging in the context of global supply chains. Dell, GM, Sun, and Nike are examples of channel master organizations for supply chains (Gaonkar & Viswanadham, 2004).

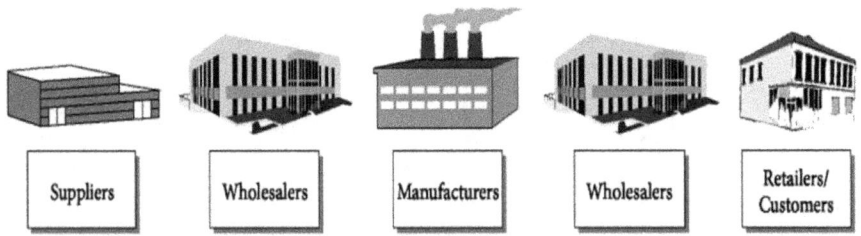

| Suppliers | Wholesalers | Manufacturers | Wholesalers | Retailers/ Customers |

Figure 10: Supply chain of a product

Various sources of power enable a leader to exercise influence over others (Nye, 2010). In the same way, a channel master's typical sources of power are its intimate customer knowledge, ownership of a strong brand name, and its ability to create ultimate demand for the supply chain (Rice & Hoppe, 2002). A channel master is a supply chain member organization that has compelling control over the sales of the product. Product manufacturers with well-known brands typically are channel masters in supply chains.

However, for many products, the power has now shifted towards powerful retailers, acting as channel masters of their supply chains (APICS, 2019). Walmart is an example of such a retailer that acts as a channel master for supply chains of many consumer products (Ayers & Odegaard, 2008).

A channel master, like other organizations, can be part of many supply chains. However, it is not necessary that a channel master enjoys the same influencing power in all the supply chains in which it is included. Thus, a channel master in one supply chain can be a minor player in another supply chain (BRASI, 2018). The channel master organizations are typically responsible for supply chain planning including; the selection of appropriate partners to develop a supply chain network and synchronization of activities between supply chain partners for optimal performance. (Gaonkar & Viswanadham, 2004). Channel masters take the initiative to integrate both upstream and downstream supply chains, getting supply chain member organizations to work cooperatively to lower total costs and achieve greater efficiency (Chapman, Gatewood, Arnold, & Clive, 2016). The channel master should ideally manage the end product demand and supply chain resources so that the supply chain accomplishes the best customer service at a lower cost (BRASI, 2018). The globalization of supply chains is one of the factors that has increased the risks of reconciling supply with demand in supply chains (Gaonkar & Viswanadham, 2004). It is therefore important for channel masters to employ appropriate risk management tools in managing their supply chains.

THREE DIMENSIONS OF CHANNEL MASTERS

Belt (2008) discussed the three main dimensions that characterize a channel master. These dimensions are political, economic, and planning-related dimensions. It is also possible that there is a separate channel master for a particular dimension in a supply chain. A political channel master organization has the decision-making power in a supply chain thus it dominates the management of a supply chain. Large hypermarkets like Walmart are examples of political channel masters for many consumer products. An economic channel master dominates and controls the money and other resources in a supply chain. The political and economic power generally goes together for channel masters. A planning channel master directs the traffic of organizations in a supply chain by correctly managing the physical and information flows in a supply chain (Belt, 2008). Strong channel masters must possess all these three dimensions of a channel master.

ENHANCING THE POWER OF A CHANNEL MASTER

Channel masters can strive to increase their political, economic, and planning dimensions of power to increase their overall effectiveness. A channel master's planning power can be enhanced with the use of technology related to Sales and Operations Planning, and Distribution Resource Planning (Belt, 2008). The Sales and Operations Planning (S&OP) process is a formal planning tool for organizations and is defined as, "A process to develop tactical plans that provide management the ability to strategically direct its businesses to achieve competitive advantage on a continuous basis by integrating customer-focused marketing plans for new and existing products with the management of the supply chain. The process brings together all the plans for the business (sales, marketing, development, manufacturing, sourcing, and financial) into one integrated set of plans. It is performed at least once a month and is reviewed by management at an aggregate (product family) level." (Blackstone, 2013, p. 154). Figure 11 shows the sequence of typical tasks performed in the Sales and Operations Planning (S&OP) process.

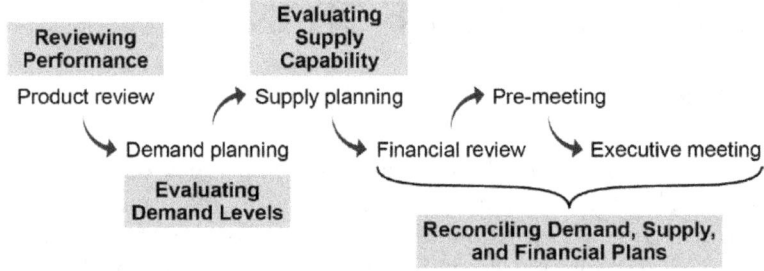

Figure 11: Sales and Operations Planning (S&OP) process

Distribution Resource Planning (DRP II) is defined as, "the extension of distribution requirements planning into the planning of the key resources contained in a distribution system (warehouse space, workforce, money, trucks, freight cars, etc.)" (Blackstone, 2013, p. 51). Figure 12 shows the nature and scope of the Distribution Requirements Planning for an organization.

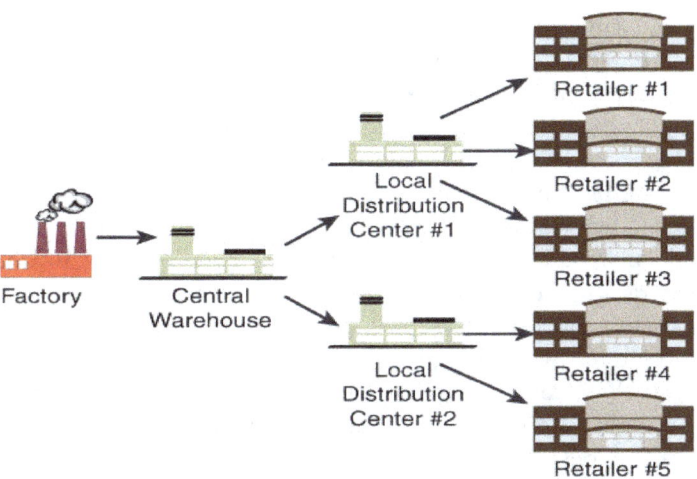

Figure 12: Distribution Requirements Planning (DRP)

A channel master can increase its economic power by implementing lean methodology to identify and eliminate waste in supply chain processes. Lean methodology eliminates waste, thus reducing operating costs and increasing profits (Belt, 2008). Lean production is defined as, "A philosophy of production that emphasizes the minimization of the amount of all the resources (including time) used in the various activities of the enterprise. It involves identifying and eliminating non-value-adding activities in design, production, supply chain management, and dealing with customers." (Blackstone, 2013, p. 60). The continuous pursuit of waste identification and elimination is the hallmark of the lean philosophy.

Fujio Cho of Toyota defined Muda (Japanese term for waste) as, "Anything other then the minimum amount of equipment, materials, part, and workers (working time) which are absolutely necessary for production." Following is the list of famous seven Wastes that can help an organization to identify and remove wastes in an organization:

1. Waste from overproduction

2. Waste of waiting time

3. Transportation waste

4. Inventory waste

5. Processing waste

6. Waste of motion

7. Waste of product defects

The increase in planning power and economic power will result in an increase in the political power of a channel master (Belt, 2008). There are many other formal supply chain planning and collaboration tools available to channel masters to increase their effectiveness. One such tool is Collaborative Planning, Forecasting, and Replenishment (CPFR) which is successfully employed in retail supply chain management (Ayers & Odegaard, 2008). CPFR is defined as, "A collaboration process whereby supply chain trading partners can jointly plan key supply chain activities from production and delivery of raw materials to production and delivery of final products to end customers. Collaboration encompasses business planning, sales forecasting, and all operations required to replenish raw materials and finished goods." (Blackstone, 2013, p. 28). Table 4 shows in CPFR there are various tasks for retailers and their suppliers. Some of these tasks are individually performed and some other tasks are performed collaboratively.

Manufacturer Tasks	Collaboration Tasks	Retailer Tasks
Strategy & Planning		
Account Planning	Collaboration Arrangement	Vendor Management
Market Planning	Joint Business Plan	Category Management
Demand & Supply Management		
Market Data Analysis	Sales Forecasting	POS Forecasting
Demand Planning	Order Planning/Forecasting	Replenishment Planning
Execution		
Production & Supply Planning	Order Generation	Buying/Re-buying
Logistics/Distribution	Order Fulfillment	Logistics/Distribution
Analysis		
Execution Monitoring	Exception Management	Store Execution
Customer Scorecard	Performance Assessment	Supplier Scorecard

Table 4: Collaborative Planning, Forecasting & Replenishment (CPFR) tasks

Channel masters can also implement the Supply Chain Operations Reference (SCOR) model to improve their supply chain operations. SCOR model, developed by Supply Chain Council (which is now part of ASCM), provides a methodology, and diagnostic and benchmarking tools that help organizations make rapid improvements in their supply chain processes (Supply Chain Council, 2012). The SCOR model has defined and is based on the six primary supply chain management processes as described in Table 5. SCOR is a cross-industry, standard diagnostic tool for supply chain management. SCOR users analyze the current state of an organization's processes and goals, quantify operational performance, and compare supply chain performance with benchmark data. SCOR also provides a set of recommended metrics to gauge the performance of various aspects of a supply chain (Blackstone, 2013). SCOR model has been successfully applied by multiple organizations belonging to various sectors of business (Ntabe, Munson, & Santa, 2015).

PROCESS	DESCRIPTION
PLAN	The Plan processes describe the activities associated with developing plans to operate the supply chain.
SOURCE	The Source processes describe the ordering (or scheduling of deliveries) and receipt of goods and services.
MAKE	Make processes describe the activities associated with the conversion of materials or the creation of the content for services.
DELIVER	The Deliver processes describe the activities associated with the creation, maintenance, and fulfillment of customer orders.
RETURN	The Return processes describe the activities associated with the reverse flow of goods.
ENABLE	The Enable processes describe the activities associated with the management of the supply chain.

Table 5: SCOR Model level 1 processes

Figure 13 shows the application of SCOR level 1 processes in a supply chain. As evident from the figure, the SCOR model applies till tier 2 of a supply chain. That is, it covers the processes of your supplier, and your supplier's supplier that is a tier 2 supplier In this same way the models applies till your customer's customer.

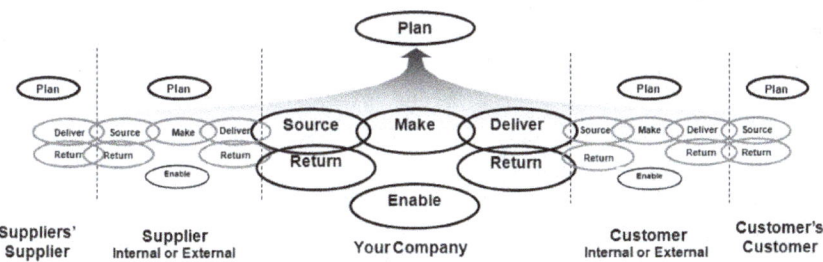

Figure 13: SCOR Model

CHANNEL MASTER CASES

As channel master examples, the salient features of Apple and Toyota supply chains are discussed in the following text. These are world-renowned organizations with global supply chains for their products. As channel masters, these organizations are effectively playing the role of a leader for their supply chains. These organizations seem to have all three sources of a channel master's leadership power. They possess intimate customer knowledge, ownership of strong brand names, and the ability to create ultimate demand for their supply chains (Rice & Hoppe, 2002). The main features of their supply chain management strategies are also discussed in this section. There are many valuable lessons to be learned from these two renowned supply chains.

Apple Inc.:

Apple Inc. has its headquarters in California, USA. The manufacturing of its renowned iPhone brand takes place at various places throughout the globe. Various components are manufactured by organizations based in many countries including Germany, USA, South Korea, China, Switzerland, and Taiwan. These component manufacturing organizations operate manufacturing facilities in multiple countries. The manufactured components are sent for assembling to two Taiwan-based organizations having production facilities in China where the final assembly of the products takes place. The assembled product is distributed and sold across the globe. (Costello, 2018). The sales and distribution of Apple's products take place via online stores, retail stores, direct sales force, wholesalers, retailers, and network carriers (Supply Chain 247, 2013).

By virtue of a strong brand name and high sales volume for its products, Apple enjoys considerable negotiation power over its supply chain partner organizations (Supply Chain 247, 2013). Strong supplier relations, strategic inventory management, and sustainability focus are the three defining features of Apple's supply chain (Ross, 2008). Apple Inc. keeps its inventory lean and has an effective inventory tracking mechanism in place. This allows Apple to remain agile and innovative in the market with respect to new product development (Ross, 2008).

One of the key features of Apple's supply chain is the maintenance of strong relationships with its supply chain partners including its suppliers (Ross, 2020). Apple Inc. has devised strict performance standards for its numerous suppliers included in Apple's supplier list. Apple's top 200 suppliers in that list account for it 98 percent of Apple's procurement (Ross, 2020). This ensures high-quality service and reliable products from its suppliers. Apple Inc. also believes in the support and development of its suppliers. Thus, Apple has offered educational and skill development programs for its suppliers. A considerable number of suppliers' employees have benefited from such training programs. Apple also maintains close communication with its suppliers and other supply chain partner organizations (Ross, 2008).

Apple is sometimes labeled as the king of outsourcing due to its effective outsourcing strategy and management of suppliers (Supply Chain 247, 2013). Its outsourcing policy of assembling many of its products in China also proved to be a successful strategy. To sum up, Apple's strong brand, high sales volume, innovation, inventory management, effective outsourcing, and long-term relationship with suppliers and other partners, are some of the key features that have enabled Apple to remain on the list of top performers in supply chain management. Thus, Apple Inc. has played very successfully a leadership role in its supply chain.

Toyota Motor Corporation:

Another good example of global supply chain management is Toyota Motor Corporation. Toyota sells its products in more than 170 countries. Toyota has 5 regional headquarters, 20 design and R&D centers, and 67 manufacturing companies worldwide (Toyota, n.d.). These manufacturing companies consist of wholly-owned companies as well as joint ventures, and contractual manufacturing facilities at various locations. A key challenge for Toyota is the design of its global production and distribution network. Toyota's strategy is to open a production facility in every market it serves. Some of its plants only serve the local market in which they are located while others are capable of serving several markets (Chopra & Meindl, 2013).

Supply chain management at Toyota is based on its operations management strategy known as the Toyota Production System (TPS). It was developed in the 1940s by Shigeo Shingo and Taiichi Ohno (Dudovskiy, n.d.). It is defined as, "a manufacturing methodology developed at Toyota that has evolved into the concepts of just-in-time and lean manufacturing" (Blackstone, 2013, p. 180). Just in time is defined as, "a philosophy of manufacturing based on planned elimination of all waste and on continuous improvement of productivity" (Blackstone, 2013, p. 88). Shigeo Shingo of Toyota Motor Corporation has identified seven types of waste in operations. These are the waste of overproduction, waste of waiting, waste of transportation, waste of inventory, waste of motion, waste of making defects, and waste of over-processing (Blackstone, 2013). Thus, the elimination of waste aspect, including the waste of overstock of inventory, is the central feature of Toyota's supply chain management strategy.

Pull production based on the Kanban system, total quality management, elimination of waste, reduction of inventory, continuous improvement, and close cooperation among supply chain partners, are the key elements of just in time system of operations management (Dudovskiy, n.d.). A system of Just in time procurement uses a few suppliers that have long-term commitments with Toyota. Longer-term contracts and relationships enable Toyota to develop and certify the process quality of the supplier. The components are delivered by suppliers on time and within quality specifications (Blackstone, 2013). A system of kanban is used to maintain a systematic physical flow through the supply chain that keeps the inventory to a minimal controlled level. Suppliers make several deliveries of smaller lots throughout the day to Toyota's production facilities (Iyer, Seshadri & Vasher, 2009). Following are some of the salient features of Toyota's supply chain management system that has made it so effective (Iyer, Seshadri, & Vasher, 2009):

• The holistic view of the whole supply chain is taken with supply chain-oriented products and facilities. Streamlined inbound and outbound logistics systems, a limited number of suppliers close to the assembly plants, and integrated supply chain and kaizen processes are some of the key features of Toyota's supply chain.

• Suppliers and dealers are considered partners of Toyota Motor Corporation.

• Close coordination and communication with suppliers, dealers, and other supply chain partners.

• The goal of overall supply chain efficiency takes precedence over individual functions and organizations.

The scope of supply chain management at Toyota Motor Corporation spans its suppliers' suppliers, the distribution channel, the dealers, and the final consumers (Iyer, Seshadri, & Vasher, 2009). The philosophy of the Toyota Production System (TPS) with its elements of just in time, Kanban, lean manufacturing, and kaizen, gives efficiency to the Toyota supply chain. This provides Toyota's supply chain an edge in the market for competing against the competition.

In this chapter, we discussed channel masters or nucleus organizations and their leadership role in managing the supply chains. However, it is the right people with leadership and other qualities in channel masters or other supply chain member organizations that are responsible for the effective display of supply chain leadership. Therefore, in the next chapter, I will discuss the leadership role of supply chain managers working for organizations in a supply chain.

Chapter 5

REQUIRED LEADERSHIP QUALITIES OF SUPPLY CHAIN MANAGERS

As discussed earlier, a supply chain is a complex concept consisting of many organizations and functions within organizations. Therefore, professionals working on supply chain management activities of an organization need to deal with multiple people, functions, and entities. The majority of the people supply chain managers deal with are not under their direct line of authority. Despite this, they need to influence the people working at various organizations or functions to achieve supply chain objectives. In other words, they need to display good leadership skills to manage supply chain management activities. This demand for leadership skills is even more for supply chain managers working in channel master organizations which need to oversee the objectives of the whole supply chain.

Not all organizations have dedicated supply chain management departments to align and coordinate supply chain management activities. Many organizations have developed, full-time or part-time, supply chain management cross-functional teams for effective and efficient management of supply chain activities. Whether operating on a full-time or a part-time basis, supply chain managers need to design, coordinate and align activities, not only within their organizational boundaries but also among partner organizations in their supply chains (APICS, 2011). They need to influence people working in various functions in their organizations like operations, warehousing, procurement, and information technology and they also need to influence outside entities like transporters, suppliers, customers, and distributors. A display of good leadership skills by supply chain managers is therefore very much needed for this purpose.

Tissayakorn, Akagi, and Song (2013) highlighted the importance of supply chain integration, customer focus, information sharing, use of the modern information technology network, and design for supply chain, for effective management of manufacturing supply chains. Supply chain professionals, therefore, need to display relevant traits and behaviors to effectively manage these supply chain-related activities. Supply chain managers need to be critical thinkers and problem solvers. They must have the ability to see the big picture, develop integrated solutions, establish contingency plans, and able to communicate the vision (Coyle, Langley,

Gibson, & Novack, 2017). Most of these required qualities relate to effective leadership skills and are mentioned in leadership literature under the headings of leadership traits (Zaccaro, 2007), leadership competencies (Tubbs & Schulz, 2006), and leadership behaviors (Yukl, Gordon & Taber, 2002). This establishes the fact that a display of good leadership skills is required from supply chain professionals. This need is even higher in cases of complex global supply chains like that of Apple Inc., and Toyota Motor Corporation.

During my Ph.D. studies, I did research on the required leadership qualities of supply chain managers. The exact title of my Ph.D. thesis was to "explore the desired leadership traits and behaviors of supply chain managers related to effective supply chain outcomes in manufacturing organizations." This chapter elaborates on the conceptual framework, research questions, research methodology, and key research findings of my study. My research can help supply chain professionals develop effective leadership skills to manage their supply chains.

CONCEPTUAL FRAMEWORK

A conceptual framework of a study sets forth the standards to define research questions and find appropriate, meaningful answers for the same. The conceptual framework connects the theories, assumptions, beliefs, and concepts behind research and presents them in a pictorial, graphical, or narrative format. The following key themes were identified for my research to explore the desired leadership traits and behaviors of supply chain managers related to effective supply chain outcomes in manufacturing organizations:

1. Leadership traits

2. Leadership behaviors

3. Leadership effectiveness

4. Supply chain effectiveness

My study used the organizational behavior approach to study the leadership qualities of supply chain managers in manufacturing organizations. The organizational behavior approach mainly uses the trait approach, the behavior approach, and the contingency approach to study leadership (Glynn & DeJordy, 2010). Figure 14 depicts the research model developed based on the organizational behavior approach to explore the desired leadership qualities of supply chain managers in manufacturing organizations for effective supply chain outcomes. According to the model, the antecedents for desired leadership qualities of a supply chain manager are the right leadership traits and the right leadership behaviors. The supply chain management environment for a manufacturing organization represents the context in which the supply chain manager is operating as a leader is operating. According to the model, the desired leadership qualities by virtue of the right traits and right behavior result in the leadership effectiveness of a supply chain manager. Enhanced leadership effectiveness of the supply chain manager thus results in effective supply chain outcomes (APICS, 2011).

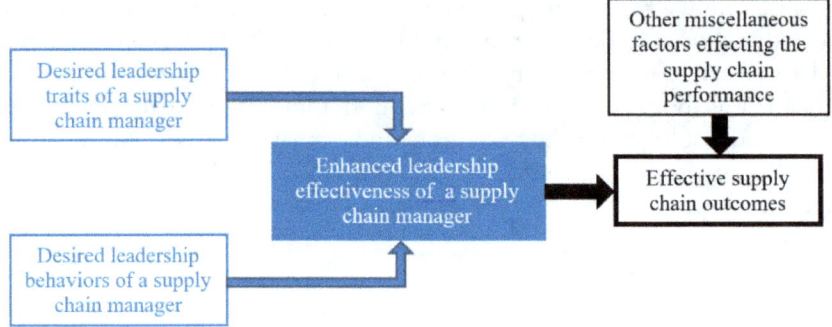

Figure 14: Research model

Other than the leadership factor, supply chain performance is also dependent upon many other factors beyond the leader's control. These factors are present within the organization as well as in the environment in which an organization is operating (Wasserman, Anand, & Nohria, 2010). Considering this, the research model also shows that other non-leadership factors contribute to effective supply chain outcomes. Thus, as per the developed research model, my research explored the desired leadership traits and behaviors of supply chain managers in manufacturing organizations.

RESEARCH QUESTIONS

The following research questions were developed for the research project to explore the desired leadership traits and behaviors of supply chain managers related to effective supply chain outcomes in manufacturing organizations:

1. How are leadership qualities for supply chain managers in manufacturing organizations related to effective supply chain outcomes?

2. What are the desired leadership traits of supply chain managers in

manufacturing organizations for effective supply chain outcomes?

3. What are the desired leadership behaviors of supply chain managers in manufacturing organizations for effective supply chain outcomes?

Research question 1 was developed to access the importance of leadership for supply chain managers specific to manufacturing organizations. Research question 2 was developed to explore the desired leadership traits of supply chain managers, whereas research question 3 was developed to explore the desired leadership behaviors of supply chain managers. The context for the study is the supply chain management environment in manufacturing organizations.

As far as the first research question is concerned, as mentioned in Chapter 3, the study confirmed that it is very important for supply chain managers in manufacturing organizations to display good leadership qualities for effective supply chain outcomes. In this chapter, I have discussed the desired leadership traits and behaviors of supply chain managers.

RESEARCH METHODOLOGY

The case study research methodology was utilized in my research. Case study research is suitable for the study of complex social phenomena in which numerous variables are in action that cannot be controlled by the researcher. Case study research can be used for exploratory, descriptive, and as well as explanatory research. It is an all-encompassing mode of inquiry that relies on multiple sources of evidence. Case study research is analogous to experiments in many ways, however, it allows the researcher to retain a holistic and real-world perspective. In case study research, the researcher may in-depth explore a program, an event, an activity, a process, or individuals (Creswell, 2003).

Figure 15 shows four types of designs for the case study research. These designs are single-case holistic designs, single-case embedded designs, multiple-case holistic designs, and multiple-case embedded designs (Yin, 2018). My research utilized the multiple-case holistic design (shown as type 3 in Figure 15) for the study in which data would be collected from more than one manufacturing organization for their supply chains. The cases for the study were the supply chain managers working for selected manufacturing organizations with effective supply chain outcomes.

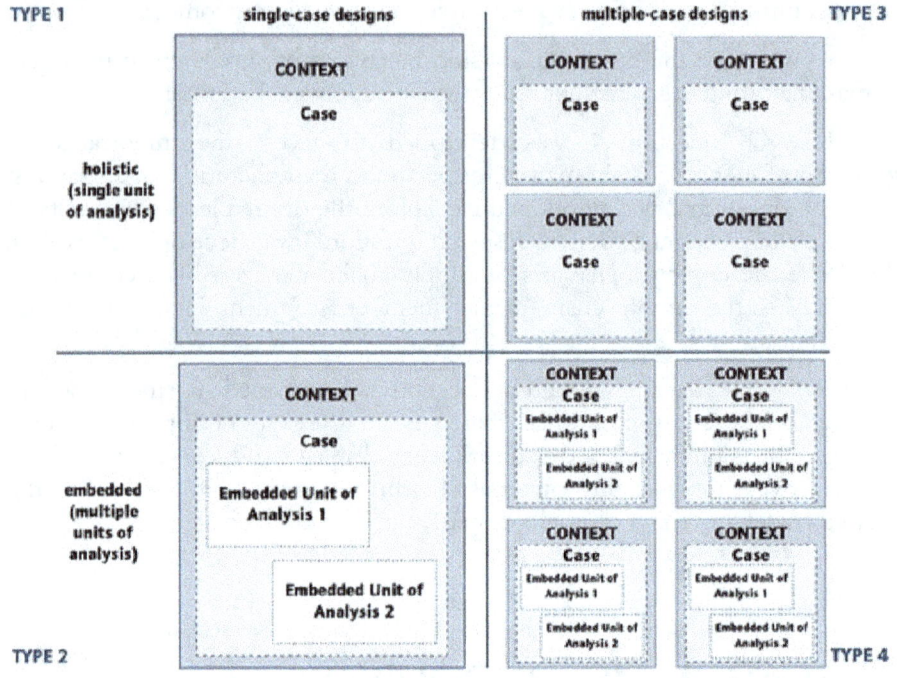

Figure 15: Basic types of designs for case studies (Yin, 2018, p. 65)

Six major sources of evidence during data collection in case study research are documentation, archival records, interviews, direct observations, participant observations, and physical artifacts (Yin, 2018). Two types of data were required from the selected organizations to conduct my study. The first type of data was general data to understand the organizations and their supply chains. This data consisted of information regarding the organization's products, major suppliers and customers, the number of employees, revenues, major supply chain processes, supply chain department structure including the reporting lines, etc. Such data was gathered from organizations' websites, brochures, annual reports, interviews, and other relevant internal or external documents. The second type of data was directly related to the research questions of the study. This data was collected to explore the desired leadership traits and leadership behaviors of supply chain managers in manufacturing organizations for effective supply chain outcomes. The major source of such data was in-depth interviews of supply chain managers of the selected organizations.

There exist five recommended approaches for case study research data analysis. These are pattern matching, explanation building, time-series analysis, logic models, and cross-case synthesis (Yin, 2018). The analytic approach of cross-case synthesis was applied for data analysis in my research project as the research had a multiple-case holistic design. The cross-case synthesis technique consists of comparison and synthesis of within-case patterns across the cases (Yin, 2018). As per this technique, data on leadership traits and leadership behaviors along with other relevant data from all three selected organizations was studied to develop individual cases for each organization. It was followed by a comparison and synthesis of the information from the three selected cases to study replicative relations across the cases. In this way, conclusions were drawn on the desired leadership traits and leadership behaviors of supply chain managers in manufacturing organizations for effective supply chain outcomes.

DESIRED LEADERSHIP TRAITS

The second research question was developed to investigate the desired leadership traits of supply chain managers in manufacturing organizations for effective supply chain outcomes. A combined coding approach (Blair, 2015) was used to analyze qualitative data to answer the research question. That is, both pre-determined template codes (Blair, 2015), as well as, open codes (Blair, 2015) generated during the data analysis phase were used to analyze the qualitative data. Leadership traits for leadership effectiveness as stated by Kirkpatrick and Locke (1991) and Zaccaro (2007) were referred to generate template codes for this purpose. Table 2 depicts the overall findings for the research question.

Most important leadership traits	• Social skills
	• Cognitive skills
	• Drive
	• Flexibility
	• Leadership motivation
	• Knowledge of the business
	• Honesty and integrity
Other important leadership traits	• Creativity/originality
	• Self-confidence
	• Charisma

Table 6: Desired Leadership Traits of Manufacturing Supply Chain Managers

The seven most important leadership traits identified for manufacturing supply chain managers were social skills, cognitive skills, drive, flexibility, leadership motivation, knowledge of the business, and honesty/integrity. Leadership traits of creativity/originality, self-confidence, and charisma were also identified but these were not as important as the aforementioned seven leadership traits.

DESIRED LEADERSHIP BEHAVIORS

The third research question was to find out the desired leadership behavior of supply chain managers. The desired leadership behavior for supply chain managers was investigated with respect to the three-dimensional hierarchical taxonomy of leadership behaviors developed by Yukl, Gordon, and Taber (2002). These three types of leadership behaviors are task behavior, relations behavior, and change behavior. Each of these meta-categories of leadership behaviors has certain specific behaviors, identified by Yukl, Gordon and Taber (2002) in their research. This three-dimensional taxonomy of leadership behavior was discussed in chapter 2 of this book; however, I am including it here again for your convenience.

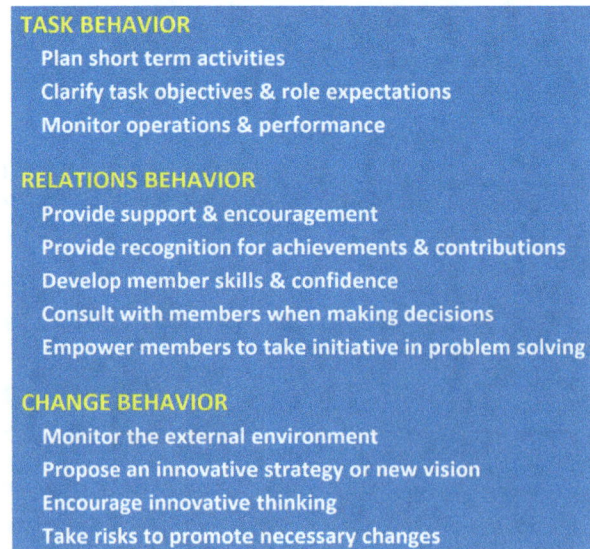

TASK BEHAVIOR
- Plan short term activities
- Clarify task objectives & role expectations
- Monitor operations & performance

RELATIONS BEHAVIOR
- Provide support & encouragement
- Provide recognition for achievements & contributions
- Develop member skills & confidence
- Consult with members when making decisions
- Empower members to take initiative in problem solving

CHANGE BEHAVIOR
- Monitor the external environment
- Propose an innovative strategy or new vision
- Encourage innovative thinking
- Take risks to promote necessary changes

Table 3: Hierarchical taxonomy of leadership behaviors

The research revealed that all these three categories of behaviors are relevant for manufacturing supply chain managers for effective supply chain outcomes. However, these behaviors were not found to be equally important. Relations behavior was found to be the most important leadership behavior followed by task behavior and then the change behavior as shown in Figure 16. The following discussion gives detailed research findings on these three meta-categories of leadership behaviors and the specific behaviors within each meta-category.

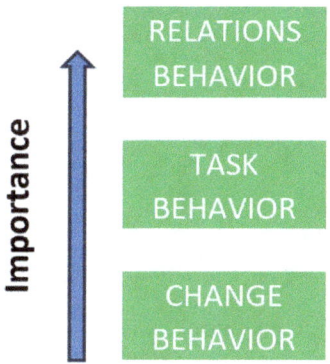

Figure 16: Relative importance of leadership behaviors

Relations Behavior:

The most important meta-category of leadership behavior for supply chain managers in manufacturing organizations for effective supply chain outcomes was found to be relations behavior. Table 4 shows that all the five specific behaviors within the relations behavior meta-category, as identified by Yukl, Gordon and Taber (2002), were found to be very important for manufacturing supply chain managers. All three case study interviewees mentioned these specific behaviors as very important for manufacturing supply chain managers for effective supply chain outcomes.

Specific relations behaviors identified as most important by all three interviewees	• Providing support and encouragement. • Providing recognition for achievements and contributions. • Developing member skills and confidence. • Consulting with members in decision-making. • Empowering members to take initiative in problem-solving.

Table 7: Desired Leadership Specific Relations Behaviors

Task Behavior:

The second most important meta-category of behaviors of supply chain managers in manufacturing organizations for effective supply chain outcomes was found to be task behavior. Two out of three specific behaviors in the task behavior meta-category, as identified by Yukl, Gordon and Taber (2002), were found to be most important for manufacturing supply chain managers. Table 8 mentions the two most important specific task behaviors as identified during the study. These specific behaviors were; clarifying task objectives and role expectations and monitoring operations and performance. The specific task behavior of planning short-term activities, as mentioned in Table 5, was also identified as important but not so important as the other two behaviors.

Most important specific task behaviors	• Clarifying task objectives and role expectations. • Monitoring operations and performance.
Other important task behavior	• Planning short-term activities.

Table 8: Desired Leadership Specific Task Behaviors of Manufacturing Supply Chain Managers

Change Behavior:

The change behavior was also identified as relevant for supply chain managers in manufacturing organizations for effective supply chain outcomes. However, the change behavior meta-category was found to be comparatively less important than relations behavior and task behavior. Two out of four specific change behaviors, as identified by Yukl, Gordon and Taber (2002), were found to be very important for manufacturing supply chain managers. Table 9 shows these two identified most important specific change behaviors as identified during the study. These specific change behaviors were; encouraging innovative thinking and monitoring the external environment. Whereas the specific behaviors of proposing an innovative strategy or new vision, and taking risks to promote necessary changes, were also identified but not as very important.

Most important specific change behaviors	• Encouraging innovative thinking. • Monitoring the external environment.
Other important change behaviors	• Proposing an innovative strategy or new vision. • Taking risks to promote necessary changes.

Table 9: Desired Leadership Specific Change Behaviors of Manufacturing Supply Chain Managers

RELATIONSHIP BETWEEN LEADERSHIP TRAITS AND BEHAVIORS

Certain findings related to identified leadership traits were found to be highly related to the findings regarding leadership behaviors for manufacturing supply chain managers for effective supply chain outcomes. The discovery of such relationships has provided triangulation for some findings of the study. The finding that relations behavior is the most important leadership behavior for manufacturing supply chain managers also matched with the research finding that social skills are one of the most important leadership traits for manufacturing supply chain managers. This relationship is also portrayed in figure 17. The presence of effective social skills as a trait help a manufacturing supply chain manager to display effective relations behavior because social skills and relations behavior are highly related.

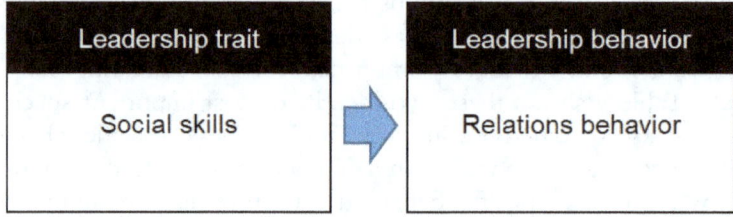

Figure 17: Relationship between social skills and relations behavior.

Change behavior, comparatively, was found to be less important than the relations behavior and task behavior for manufacturing supply chain managers for effective supply chain outcomes. This finding matched with the finding on leadership traits where the trait of creativity/originality was found to be relevant but comparatively less important than other important identified leadership traits. This is because there is a relationship between creativity/originality and the change behavior. This relationship is portrayed in figure 18. The leadership trait of creativity/originality results in new ideas of doing the business that in turn results in changes in the current business processes. This finding of comparatively less importance of leadership change behavior corresponds with the leadership trait finding of comparatively less importance of the leadership trait of creativity/originality.

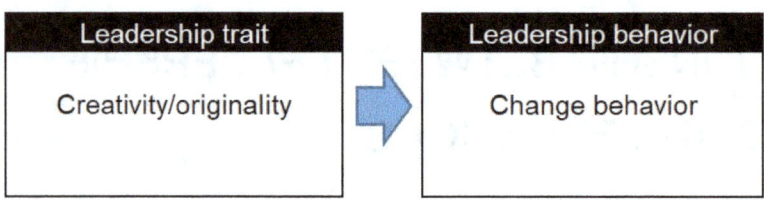

Figure 18: Relationship between creativity/originality and change behavior.

DISCUSSION ON DESIRED LEADERSHIP TRAITS

The study showed that the leadership traits of social skills, cognitive skills, drive, flexibility, leadership motivation, knowledge of the business, and honesty/integrity, are the most important traits for manufacturing supply chain managers for effective supply chain outcomes. Other relevant but comparatively less important leadership traits for manufacturing supply chain managers are creativity/originality, self-confidence, and charisma. Figure 19 shows that five out of a total seven most important leadership traits identified in the study for manufacturing supply chain managers were also identified as significant traits for leaders in general by Kirkpatrick and Locke (1991) in their study. These common leadership traits were drive, leadership motivation, honesty/integrity, cognitive ability, and knowledge of the business.

Figure 19: A comparison of Kirkpatrick and Locke (1991) identified significant leadership traits and most important desired leadership traits of supply chain managers.

This comparison of leadership traits in Figure 19 implies that most of the requirements of desired leadership traits are common between manufacturing supply chain managers and other leaders in general. This is quite plausible as supply chain managers are part of the overall community of leaders functioning in various contexts. Apart from these five common leadership traits, the two additional most important leadership traits for manufacturing supply chain managers as leaders are social skills, and flexibility. The trait of social skills is required by manufacturing supply chain managers to display leadership relations behavior. The relations behavior was found to be the most important leadership behavior in the study for the manufacturing supply chain managers. Whereas, the trait of flexibility is directly related to certain important supply chain management tasks that are later discussed in this chapter. The leadership trait of self-confidence was not identified in the category of most important leadership traits during the study, however, this does not mean this trait is not required at all by the supply chain managers. Self-confidence is a required trait but not identified as the most important as the other seven identified traits during the study.

Table 10 shows some important supply chain management tasks identified by Coyle, Langley, Gibson and Novack (2017) in relation to the desired leadership traits of manufacturing supply chain managers identified in the study.

SUPPLY CHAIN MANAGEMENT TASKS	SUPPORTING LEADERSHIP TRAITS
Critical thinking and problem-solving	Cognitive ability, and knowledge of the business
Ability to see the big picture	Knowledge of the business
Develop integrated solutions	Cognitive ability, knowledge of the business, and flexibility
Establish contingency plans	Cognitive ability, knowledge of the business, and flexibility
Communicate the vision	Social skills, and knowledge of the business

Table 10: Relation Between Supply Chain Management Tasks (Coyle, Langley, Gibson & Novack, 2017) and Desired Leadership Traits of Manufacturing Supply Chain Managers

The critical thinking and problem-solving tasks are expected to be supported by the traits of cognitive ability, and knowledge of the business of the supply chain managers. The ability to see the big picture is expected to be supported by the trait related to the knowledge of the business of the supply chain manager. The tasks of developing integrated solutions and establishing contingency plans are expected to be supported by the traits of cognitive ability, knowledge of the business, and flexibility. The task of communicating a vision is expected to be supported by the traits of social skills and knowledge of the business.

The remaining three identified most important leadership traits of drive, leadership motivation, and honesty/integrity are not mentioned in Table 10. These traits can be considered basic enablers that are required by all types of leaders for their leadership effectiveness. A leader operating in any context can be ineffective if he or she is void of basic traits like drive, leadership motivation, and honesty/integrity.

Considering the above discussion, it is concluded that the most important leadership traits for manufacturing supply chain managers for effective supply chain outcomes are social skills, cognitive skills, drive, flexibility, leadership motivation, knowledge of the business, and honesty/integrity. Other important leadership traits for manufacturing supply chain managers are creativity/originality, self-confidence, and charisma. Most of these leadership traits are found to be directly related to the major supply chain management tasks identified in the supply chain management literature. Thus supply chain managers in manufacturing organizations must make conscious efforts to develop or further improve on these leadership traits to improve their leadership effectiveness as supply chain managers. Various developmental efforts including participation in management and leadership development programs can help manufacturing supply chain managers in this regard.

DISCUSSION ON DESIRED LEADERSHIP BEHAVIORS

The study showed that all three meta-categories of leadership behaviors, that are, relations behavior, task behavior, and change behavior (Yukl, Gordon & Taber, 2002) are relevant for manufacturing supply chain managers for effective supply chain outcomes. Relations behavior was however found to be the most important leadership behavior for manufacturing supply chain managers followed by task behavior and change behavior. The finding that relations behavior is the most important leadership behavior for manufacturing supply chain managers also matched with the other research finding on desired leadership traits and the important supply chain management related task of relationship management identified in the literature (Coyle, Langley, Gibson & Novack, 2017). This relationship is portrayed in Figure 20.

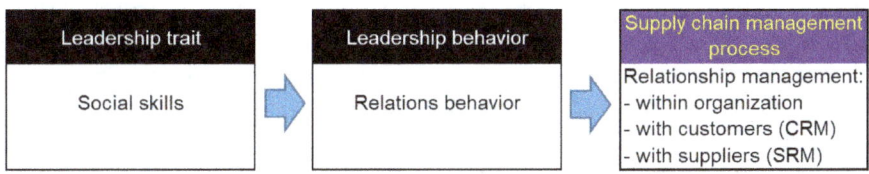

Figure 20: Relationship between social skills, relations behavior, and supply chain relationship management.

The presence of effective social skills as a trait helps a manufacturing supply chain manager to display effective relations behavior. Effective display of relations behavior will, in turn, help a manufacturing supply chain manager in relationship management with entities inside and outside the organization. Relationship management within the organization is with organizational internal functional areas including marketing, sales, operations/manufacturing, and accounting/finance. Relationship management outside the organization involves outside entities like vendors, customers, transporters, third-party logistics providers (3PLs), and other service providers (Coyle, Langley, Gibson & Novack, 2017). Customer relationship management (CRM) and supplier relationship management (SRM) are two major groups of relationship management activities with outside entities in managing the supply chains (APICS, 2019). These two activities must be supported by the relations behavior of manufacturing supply chain managers.

According to the study results, after relations behavior, the second important meta-category of leadership behavior is task behavior. The meta-category of change behavior is found to be relatively less important than both the relations behavior and the task behavior. This finding also matched with the finding on leadership traits where the trait creativity/originality was found to be relevant but comparatively less important than other important identified traits like social skills. This is because there is a relationship between creativity/originality and change behavior as portrayed in figure 21.

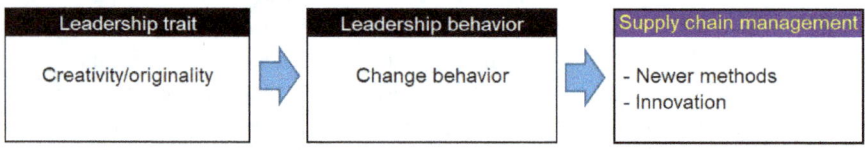

Figure 21: Relationship between creativity/originality, change behavior, and innovation in supply chain management.

Creativity/originality trait in a supply chain manager is related to the change behavior. The change behavior of the supply chain manager, in turn, will bring about changes in the current work processes in supply chain management. The research finding that the change behavior is comparatively less significant for manufacturing supply chain managers is also plausible. This is because changes and innovations are not so frequent in any area of management including in supply chain management. Useful changes in business practices are always needed as these help businesses remain competitive in the market by increasing their effectiveness and efficiency. However, practically speaking, innovations in business practices are not possible on a daily basis. In comparison, managing relationships and managing supply chain management routine tasks is an ongoing process.

Considering the above discussion, it is concluded the most important leadership behavior for manufacturing supply chain managers for effective supply chain outcomes is the relations behavior followed by the task behavior and the change behavior. The ranking of the three meta-categories of leadership behaviors for manufacturing supply chain managers along with specific leadership behaviors (Yukl, Gordon & Taber, 2002) is portrayed in Table 11.

RANKING	META-CATEGORY	SPECIFIC BEHAVIOR
1st	Relations behavior	• Providing support and encouragement. • Providing recognition for achievements and contributions. • Developing member skills and confidence. • Consulting with members in decision-making. • Empowering members to take initiative in problem-solving.
2nd	Task behavior	• Clarifying task objectives and role expectations. • Monitoring operations and performance.
3rd	Change behavior	• Encouraging innovative thinking. • Monitoring the external environment.

Table 11: Desired Leadership Behaviors for Manufacturing Supply Chain Managers

The table can be very useful for manufacturing supply chain managers for improving their leadership behavior for effective supply chain outcomes. Especially the last column of the table that provides specific guidance in terms of desired leadership behaviors. Such information can also be used by training departments of progressive manufacturing organizations for designing supply chain management related developmental programs for their organizations.

CONCLUSION

This book discussed in detail the leadership for managing the supply chains. Organizations throughout the world have recognized the importance of managing their supply chains effectively and efficiently to gain a competitive advantage in the marketplace. A supply chain is a complex phenomenon associated with multiple functions, organizations, and processes to deliver goods and services to customers. A channel master is a dominant organization in a supply chain that enjoys compelling control over the sales of the product. A channel master organization plays a leadership role in a supply chain as it exerts its influence on other organizations to seek cooperation for aligning supply chain management activities for the whole chain. There are political, economic, and planning dimensions that characterize a channel master's role in a supply chain.

Supply chain professionals have to deal with multiple people at various entities to achieve supply chain goals. This is especially true for supply chain managers working for channel master organizations. Therefore, managing supply chains effectively requires excellent leadership skills on the part of supply chain professionals. My Ph.D. research attempted to explore the desired leadership skills of manufacturing supply chain managers in terms of desired leadership traits and behaviors for effective supply chain outcomes. Three research questions were developed and explored during the research. The study successfully filled the knowledge gap in the leadership and supply chain management literature regarding the desired leadership traits and behaviors of manufacturing supply chain managers. The following conclusions were drawn from the research project with respect to the three research questions developed for the study.

It is concluded that leadership qualities are very important for supply chain managers working in manufacturing organizations for effective supply chain outcomes. The most important leadership traits for manufacturing supply chain managers are social skills, cognitive skills, drive, flexibility, leadership motivation, knowledge of the business, and honesty/integrity. Other important leadership traits for manufacturing supply chain managers are self-confidence, creativity/originality, and charisma. The most important leadership behavior for manufacturing supply chain managers for effective supply chain outcomes is the relations behavior followed by the task behavior and then the change behavior.

The most important specific relations behaviors for manufacturing supply chain managers are: providing support and encouragement; providing recognition for achievements and contributions; developing member skills and confidence; consulting with members in decision-making; and empowering members to take initiative in problem-solving. The most important specific task behaviors for manufacturing supply chain managers are: clarifying task objectives and role expectations; and monitoring operations and performance. The most important specific change behaviors for manufacturing supply chain managers are: encouraging innovative thinking; and monitoring the external environment.

The conclusions drawn from my research can be used by aspiring supply chain managers and their manufacturing sector organizations for leadership development interventions of supply chain professionals. The study can also be used by universities and management training organizations to develop effective training and educational programs targeting manufacturing sector supply chain managers. The most important desired leadership traits and behaviors identified in the study must be considered in designing such leadership developmental programs for manufacturing supply chain managers.

REFERENCES

Allden, M., Niemann, W., & Kotzé, T. (2018). Industry expectations of supply chain management graduates: Perspectives from third-party logistics providers in South Africa. Journal of Transport and Supply Chain Management, 12(1), p. 1-14.

Antai, I., & Olson, H. (2013). Interaction: a new focus for supply chain vs supply chain competition. International Journal of Physical Distribution & Logistics Management, 43(7) p. 511 - 528.

APICS. (2011). Supply chain management fundamentals. (Certified supply chain professional learning system). Chicago, United States: APICS.

APICS. (2014). Supply chain manager competency model. Chicago, United States: APICS.

APICS. (2019). APICS CSCP learning system. Chicago, United States: APICS.

AuVitronics Limited. (n.d.). Retrieved from https://auvitronics.com/

Ayers, J. B. & Odegaard, M. A. (2008). Retail supply chain management (1st ed.). USA: Auerbach Publications.

Barrasa, A. (2003). Hierarchical taxonomy of leadership behavior: Antecedents, structure, and influence in work groups effectiveness. Retrieved from https://scholar.google.com.pk/scholar?cluster=17133845547482386887&hl=en&as_sdt=0,5#d=gs_cit&u=%2Fscholar%3Fq%3Dinfo%3Ax5EYFr-lx-0J%3Ascholar.google.com%2F%26output%3Dcite%26scirp%3D0%26scfhb%3D1%26hl%3Den

Belt, B. (2008, June 15). The three dimensions of channel masters. Retrieved from http://www.heenan.com.au/wp-content/uploads/2009/03/lettech67anglais.pdf

Blair, E. (2015). A reflexive exploration of two qualitative data coding techniques. Journal of Methods and Measurement in the Social Sciences, 6(1), p. 14 - 29.

BRASI. (2018). Planning. (Certificate in supply chain and operations management learning system). Stroudsburg, United States: BRASI.

Burta, F. S. (2018). Supply chain management and performance: Framework for strategic decision making. The Annals of the University of Oradea, 26(1), p. 430 438.

Business Edge, IFC. (n.d). Influencing [PowerPoint slides]

Chapman, S., Gatewood, A. K., Arnold, T. K., & Clive, L. (2016) Introduction of materials management. Introduction to materials management (p. 13 – 29). Pearson Higher Ed.

Chopra, S. & Meindl, P. (2013). Supply chain management: Strategy, planning, and operation (10th Ed.). Pearson Education India.

Cîrstea, C., & Constantinescu, D. (2012). Debating about situational leadership. Management and Marketing, 1(1), p. 53-58.

Costello S. (July 14, 2018). Life Wire. Where is the iPhone made? Retrieved August 18, 2018 from https://www.lifewire.com/where-is-the-iphone-made-1999503

Coyle J. J., Langley C. J., Gibson B. J., Novack R. A., & Bardi E. J. (2009). Supply Chain Management. A Logistics Perspective (8th ed.). Ohio, USA: Cengage Learning.

Coyle J. J., Langley C. J., Gibson B. J., & Novack R. A. (2017). Supply chain management. A logistics perspective (10th ed.). Ohio, USA: Cengage Learning.

Creswell J. W. (2003). Research design: Qualitative, quantitative and mixed methods approaches (2nd ed.). USA: Sage Publications, Inc.

Crook, T. R., Giunipero, L., Reus, T. H., Handfield, R., & Williams, S. K. (2008). Antecedents and outcomes of supply chain effectiveness: An exploratory investigation. Journal of Managerial Issues, 20(2) p. 161-177.

Dixon, M., & Hart, L. (2010). The impact of Path-Goal leadership styles on work group effectiveness and turnover intention. Journal of Managerial Issues, 22(1), 52-69. Retrieved from http://www.jstor.org/stable/25822515

Dudovskiy, J. (n.d.). Life Wire. Supply chain management in Toyota Motor Corportion. Retrieved August 3, 2020 from https://research-methodology.net/supply-chain-management-toyota-motor-corporation/

Germain, M. L. (2012). Traits and skills theories as the nexus between leadership and expertise: Reality or fallacy? Performance Improvement, 51(5), p. 32-39.

Glynn, M. A., & DeJordy, R. (2010). Leadership through an organization behavior lens: A look at the last half century of research. In Nohria, N.

Editor & Khurana, R Editor (Eds.), Handbook of leadership theory and practice (p. 119 - 158). Boston, Massachusetts: Harvard Business Press.

Gaonkar, R., & Viswanadham, N. (2004, April). A conceptual and analytical framework for the management of risk in supply chains. In IEEE International Conference on Robotics and Automation, 2004. Proceedings. ICRA'04. 2004 (Vol. 3, pp. 2699-2704). IEEE.

Goleman, D. (2000). Leadership that gets results. Harvard business review, 78(2), p. 4-17.

Guillen, M. F. (2010). Classical sociological approaches to the study of leadership. In Nohria, N. Editor & Khurana, R Editor (Eds.), Handbook of leadership theory and practice (p. 223 - 238). Boston, Massachusetts: Harvard Business Press.

Hackman, J.R. (2010). What is this thing called leadership? In Nohria, N. Editor & Khurana, R Editor (Eds.), Handbook of leadership theory and practice (p. 107 - 118). Boston, Massachusetts: Harvard Business Press.

Hersey, P. & Blanchard, K.H. (1969). Life cycle theory of leadership. Training & Development Journal, 23(5), p. 26-34.

Hollenbeck, G. P., McCall Jr, M. W., & Silzer, R. F. (2006). Leadership competency models. The Leadership Quarterly, 17(4), 398-413.

Hoppe, R. M. (2001). Outlining a future of supply chain management-coordinated supply networks (Doctoral dissertation, Massachusetts Institute of Technology).

Iyer, A. V., Seshadri, S. & Vasher, R. (2009). Toyota supply chain management (1st ed.). New York, USA: McGraw Hill Education.

Johnson, A., & Luthans, F. (1990). The relationship between leadership and management: An Empirical assessment. Journal of Managerial Issues, 2(1), 13-25. Retrieved from http://www.jstor.org/stable/40603704

Kirkpatrick, S. A. & Locke, E. A. (1991). Leadership: Do traits matter? Academy of Management, Vol. 5 (2), p. 48-60. Retrieved from https://www.jstor.org/stable/4165007

Lorsch, J. (2010). A contingency theory of leadership. In Nohria, N. Editor & Khurana, R Editor (Eds.), Handbook of leadership theory and practice (p. 411 - 432). Boston, Massachusetts: Harvard Business Press.

Luthans, F. (2008). Organizational Behavior. (11th ed.). New York, USA: McGraw Hill.

Mikhail, N. (2018, December). Tomorrow's CEOs will come from an unlikely place: The supply chain. Fortune. Retrieved from http://fortune.com/2018/12/11/ceo-supply-chain/

Mumford, T. V., Campion, M. A., & Morgeson, F. P. (2007). The leadership skills strataplex: Leadership skill requirements across organizational levels. The Leadership Quarterly, 18(2), 154-166.

Nitsche, B. (2018). Unravelling the complexity of supply chain volatility management. Logistics, 2(3), p. 14.

Nohria, N. & Khurana, R. (2010). Handbook of leadership theory and practice. Boston, Massachusetts: Harvard Business Press.

Ntabe, E. N., LeBel, L., Munson, A. D., & Santa-Eulalia, L. A. (2015). A systematic literature review of the supply chain operations reference (SCOR) model application with special attention to environmental issues. International Journal of Production Economics, 169, p. 310-332.

Nye, J. S. (2010). Leading change: Power and leadership. In Nohria, N. Editor & Khurana, R Editor (Eds.), Handbook of leadership theory and practice (p. 305 - 332). Boston, Massachusetts: Harvard Business Press.

Pitman P. H. and Atwater, J. B. (Eds.), APICS dictionary (15th ed.). Chicago, United States: APICS.

Podolny, J. M., Khurana, R. & Besharov, M. L. (2010). Revisiting the meaning of leadership. In Nohria, N. Editor & Khurana, R Editor (Eds.), Handbook of leadership theory and practice (p. 65 - 106). Boston, Massachusetts: Harvard Business Press.

Quantitative versus Qualitative Research or both?. (n.d). Retrieved 2019, March 19 from http://www.huparis.edu.eu/moodle/course/view.php?id=464

Rice, J. B., & Hoppe, R. M. (2001). Supply chain vs. supply chain: The hype and the reality. Supply Chain Management Review, 5(5), p. 46 - 54.

Rice, J. B. & Hoppe, R. M. (2002). Network master & three dimensions of supply network coordination: an introductory essay. Supply Chain Management Review. Retrieved from http://web.mit.edu/supplychain/repository/network_v25.pdf

Robbins, S. P., & Mary, C. (2016). Being an effective leader. Management (13th ed.) (p. 522 - 553). Essex, England: Pearson Education Limited.

Rogers, D., & Leuschner, R. (2004). Supply chain management: Retrospective and prospective. Journal of Marketing Theory and Practice, 12(4), 60-65. Retrieved from http://www.jstor.org/stable/40470179

Ross, L. (June 30, 2020). How the Apple supply chain stays top ranked in the world. Retrieved from https://www.thomasnet.com/insights/apple-supply-chain/

Supply Chain 247. (September 2, 2013). Is Apple's supply chain really no. 1? Retrieved from https://www.supplychain247.com/article/is_apples_supply_chain_reall y_the_no._1_a_case_study

Supply Chain Council. (2012). Supply Chain Operations Reference Model. USA.

Schoemaker, P. J., Krupp, S., & Howland, S. (2013). Strategic leadership: The essential skills. Harvard business review, 91(1), p. 131-134.

Southampton Education School. (2012, August 14). Analyzing your interviews [Video file]. Retrieved from https://www.youtube.com/watch?v=59GsjhPolPs

Tissayakorn, K., Akagi, F., & Song, Y. (2013). An integrated supply chain management to manufacturing industries. International Journal of Mechanical and Mechatronics Engineering, 7(12), p. 3138-3141.

Toyota. (n.d.). Where are we today. Retrieved July 31, 2020, from https://www.toyota-europe.com/world-of-toyota/this-is-toyota/toyota-in-the-world

Tubbs, S. L., & Schulz, E. (2006). Exploring a taxonomy of global leadership competencies and meta-competencies. Journal of American Academy of Business, 8(2), p. 29-34.

Vitae. (n.d.). Research projects stakeholders. Retrieved from https://www.vitae.ac.uk/doing-research/leadership-development-for-principal-investigators-pis/leading-a-research-project/applying-for-research-funding/research-project-stakeholders

Wasserman, N., Anand, B. & Nohria, N. (2010). When does leadership matter? A contingent opportunities view of CEO leadership. In Nohria, N. Editor & Khurana, R Editor (Eds.), Handbook of leadership theory and practice (p. 27 - 64). Boston, Massachusetts: Harvard Business Press.

Weirich, H., Cannice, M. V., & Koontz, H. (2008). Management: A global and entrepreneurial perspective. New Delhi.

Yin, R. K. (2018). Case study research and applications: Design and methods (6th ed.). California, USA: Sage publications.

Yukl, G. (1989). Managerial leadership: A review of theory and research.

Journal of Management, Vol. 15 (2), p. 251- 289. DOI: 10.1177/014920638901500207

Yukl, G., Gordon, A., & Taber, T. (2002). A hierarchical taxonomy of leadership behavior: Integrating a half century of behavior research. Journal of Leadership & Organizational Studies, 9(1), p.15-32.

Zaccaro, S. J. (2007). Trait-based perspectives of leadership. American psychologist, 62(1), p. 6 -16.

ABOUT THE AUTHOR

Dr. Adeel Zeerak was born on December 9, 1968, in Karachi, a sprawling, cosmopolitan city and the business hub of Pakistan. He received his early education at St. Paul's English High School in Karachi. He then joined D J Science College in Karachi to receive his 'intermediate' college education. He graduated with a Mechanical Engineering degree from NED University of Engineering and Technology, Karachi, in 1993. He did his Master in Business Administration (MBA) with a dual specialization in Marketing and Finance from the Institute of Business Administration (IBA), Karachi, Pakistan, in 1999. He received his Ph.D. degree in International Leadership from Horizons University in Paris, France. Dr. Adeel Zeerak is also a 'Certified Supply Chain Professional' (CSCP) from APICS, USA. He has earned many other professional certifications from world-renowned organizations related to the field of supply chain management. Dr. Zeerak has attended numerous management and technical training programs including a four-week training held in Malaysia on 'Workshop on Green-Productivity for trainers and consultants'. The training was sponsored by the Asian Productivity Organization, Tokyo, Japan.

During his 25-plus years of rich employment experience, Dr. Adeel Zeerak has undertaken a variety of work roles in the industry and academia. While working as a management consultant at the Pakistan Institute of Management (PIM), Dr. Adeel Zeerak has developed and conducted various trainings throughout Pakistan predominantly in the fields of General Management and Operations Management. He has also provided consultancy services to various organizations in the areas of General and Operations Management. Dr. Adeel Zeerak has also served the manufacturing sector of Pakistan in various capacities for more than 10 years. During this period, he was mainly involved with the automotive sector.

Dr. Adeel Zeerak is the author of many books on various topics. His books are available at renowned online bookselling platforms throughout the world including www.amazaon.com. Dr. Adeel Zeerak is also a great admirer of Martial Arts. He is himself a Black Belt holder of the world-renowned Japanese martial art of Shotokan Karate. His other hobbies include swimming and reading. He maintains a personal library with a collection on various topics including Engineering, Medical and General Sciences, Management, Economics, Finance, Martial Arts, Mathematics, History, and Religion.

The following book is available at www.amazon.com, in case you are interested to know more about leadership.

www.ingramcontent.com/pod-product-compliance
Lightning Source LLC
Chambersburg PA
CBHW072342290526
45794CB00002B/982

9798857231616